HOW TO

USE QUICKEN

Manage Income, Expenses, Investments, and

Budgets with Ease

MAXWELL S. RYDER

COPYRIGHT @ 2025. ALL RIGHTS RESERVED

DISCLAIMER

This book is an independent resource and is not affiliated with, endorsed by, or sponsored by Quicken Inc. The content is for informational purposes only and should not be considered financial, legal, or professional advice. While efforts have been made to ensure accuracy, the author and publisher are not liable for any errors, omissions, or outcomes from using this material. Readers should consult a financial professional for specific guidance.

DEDICATION

*To everyone striving for financial clarity and control—
this book is for you.*

*To beginners taking their first steps in budgeting and
personal finance—may this guide simplify your journey.*

*And to my family and friends, whose unwavering support
and encouragement fuel my passion for writing—thank
you.*

HOW TO USE THIS BOOK

Managing your finances with Quicken should feel empowering, not overwhelming. That's why this book is structured to guide you step by step, no matter where you are in your financial journey. Whether you're a complete beginner or looking to master Quickens advanced features, this book is designed to be practical, easy to follow, and immediately useful.

Here's how to make the most of it:

1. Start Where You Are

If you're completely new to Quicken, begin with the basics in Chapter 1: Quicken 101. This section will introduce you to the software, explain why it's a powerful financial tool, and help you set realistic goals for managing your money. If you already have some experience with Quicken but want to refine your skills, feel free to jump to sections that address your specific needs—whether it's budgeting, investment tracking, debt management, or advanced financial reports. Each chapter is written to be self-contained, so you can skip ahead or revisit topics as needed.

2. Follow Step-by-Step Instructions

Throughout the book, you'll find clear, actionable steps that walk you through Quickens features. From setting up your accounts to automating transactions, these steps ensure that you don't just learn *about* Quicken—you actually implement it in a way that makes your financial management easier.

3. Apply What You Learn Immediately

Each chapter includes real-world examples, practical tips, and strategies that you can apply to your own finances. The best way to absorb the information is to try it out in Quicken as you go. Open the software, follow along, and start seeing the benefits in real time.

4. Use This as a Reference Guide

Even after you've finished reading, this book is meant to be a resource you can return to anytime. Whether you need a refresher on how to set up budgets, track your spending, or create detailed financial reports, you'll find answers easily. Keep this book handy and revisit sections whenever you need guidance.

5. Customize Quicken to Fit Your Life

One of the best things about Quicken is that it's flexible—it works for personal budgets, business finances, investment tracking, and more. This book will show you how to customize categories, set up reminders, automate transactions, and generate reports that align with your unique financial situation.

6. Commit to Long-Term Success

Financial management isn't a one-time task—it's a habit. The strategies in this book will help you stay organized, make better financial decisions, and build wealth over time. By consistently using Quicken, you'll eliminate financial stress, gain clarity over your money, and take control of your future.

Now, it's time to get started. Open the next chapter and take the first step toward financial mastery with Quicken!

TABLES OF CONTENTS

INTRODUCTION 13

CHAPTER 1...15

WHY QUICKEN 15

    Understanding Quicken and Its Benefits...16

    The Importance of Personal Finance Management 17

        Key Features to Simplify Money Management.................................18

CHAPTER 2...20

GETTING STARTED WITH QUICKEN 20

    Installing and Setting Up Quicken...20

    Creating and Managing Your Quicken Account 21

    Navigating the Quicken Dashboard...22

    Manual Entry vs. Automatic Sync...22

    Organizing Finances with Categories...23

CHAPTER 3...24

MANAGING YOUR DAY-TO-DAY FINANCES 24

Tracking Income and Expenses...28

    Why Tracking Your Income Matters..................................28

    Why Expense Tracking is Crucial...................................29

    Types of Expenses..30

    How to Track Your Income and Expenses.........................31

Building and Maintaining a Budget...33

    Why Budgeting Matters..33

    Steps to Building a Budget..34

    Maintaining a Budget for Long-Term Success....................37

Managing Bills, Payments, and Reminders................................39

    Why Effective Bill Management Matters...........................39

    Steps to Efficiently Manage Bills and Payments................40

Handling Debts and Loans Efficiently.....................................43

    Why Efficient Debt Management Matters.........................44

    Steps to Handling Debt and Loans Efficiently...................44

CHAPTER 4...50

ADVANCED FEATURES FOR EXPERIENCED USERS 50

Tracking and Managing Investments.......................................51

    Why Tracking Investments is Important...........................51

    Steps to Effectively Track and Manage Investments...........52

Generating and Customizing Financial Reports 57

    Why Financial Reports Matter 58

    Types of Financial Reports 58

    How to Generate Financial Reports...61

    Customizing Your Reports 63

Tax Planning Made Simple 64

    Why Tax Planning is Important..65

    Key Concepts in Tax Planning 65

    Basic Tax Planning Strategies 67

    Using Tax Software for Simple Planning...70

Personalizing Categories and Tags...70

    What are Categories and Tags? 71

    Why Personalize Categories and Tags?...71

    How to Personalize Categories and Tags in Quicken........................72

CHAPTER 5...**76**

OPTIMIZING YOUR FINANCIAL STRATEGY **76**

Using Forecasting Tools for Smarter Planning 77

    Why Financial Forecasting Matters...77

    How Forecasting Tools Work in Quicken 78

    Steps to Use Forecasting Tools Effectively......................................79

Maximizing the Benefits of Forecasting 79

Effective Debt Reduction Techniques 80

Setting and Achieving Retirement and Savings Goals 85

Quicken for Small Business Owners 89

CHAPTER 6 ....**95**

TRANSITIONING TO QUICKEN **95**

Adapting to a Digital Financial System 96

Making the Most of Quickens Capabilities 99

CHAPTER 7 ....**104**

AVOIDING COMMON MISTAKES **104**

The Most Frequent Quicken Errors and How to Fix Them 105

Best Practices for Efficient and Error-Free Management 110

CHAPTER 8 ....**118**

USER SUCCESS STORIES **118**

Real-Life Case Studies of Quicken Users 118

Case Study 1: Sarah, A Busy Professional Who Paid Off Her Debt....119

Case Study 2: Mark and Lisa, Newlyweds Building Their First Home
....120

Case Study 3: James, A Freelance Graphic Designer Managing Irregular Income 121

Case Study 4: Jessica, A Small Business Owner Keeping Track of Cash Flow 122

Case Study 5: Tom, A Retiree Planning for the Future.........................123

CHAPTER 9...**125**

TROUBLESHOOTING AND BEST PRACTICES..........................**125**

Resolving Common Issues and Errors.......................................126

Protecting Your Financial Data 131

Exploring the Quicken Mobile App 137

CHAPTER 10...**143**

FINANCIAL HEALTH CHECK UP **143**

Evaluating Your Finances and Making Improvements 144

CHAPTER 11...**149**

PRO TIPS FOR POWER USERS **149**

Customizing Reports for In-Depth Analysis 150

Automating Financial Tasks for Efficiency................................154

Syncing Devices and Cloud Integration 160

CONCLUSION 166

INTRODUCTION

Imagine this: It's the end of the month, and you're staring at your bank statement with a sinking feeling in your stomach. You were sure you had everything under control, but somehow, your expenses once again spiraled beyond what you expected. You scroll through transactions, trying to piece together where your money went—subscriptions you forgot to cancel, impulse purchases, and bills that snuck up on you. Sound familiar?

You're not alone. Managing money is one of the biggest struggles for individuals and families alike. No one teaches us how to budget in school. We're expected to just "figure it out" as we go. But what if there was a better way? What if you could track every dollar, plan for your future, and actually feel in control of your financial life?

This is where Quicken comes in.

Quicken isn't just another budgeting tool—it's your financial roadmap. It's the system that helps you stop living paycheck to paycheck, avoid late fees, and build real wealth. But here's the truth: most people who try to use financial software give up because they don't know where to start. They get overwhelmed with the setup, confused by the features, and before long, they abandon the very tool that could change their financial future.

That won't be you.

This book is designed to take you by the hand and walk you through Quicken, step by step. Whether you're a total beginner or someone looking to master the more advanced features, you'll find easy-to-follow guidance, real-world examples, and practical tips to make managing money effortless. By the time you finish this book, you'll not only understand Quicken—you'll be using it with confidence to budget smarter, track your investments, and take full control of your financial future. You deserve financial clarity. You deserve to feel secure. You deserve a system that works for you, not against you.

By the last page of this book, you'll no longer be that person staring at their bank statement in frustration. Instead, you'll be the person who knows exactly where their money is going, how to make it work harder for them, and how to build lasting financial success.

CHAPTER 1

WHY QUICKEN

Managing personal finances can be overwhelming, especially with multiple income sources, bills, loans, and savings accounts to track. Without a structured system, it's easy to lose sight of where your money is going, leading to poor financial decisions, late payments, and missed savings opportunities. This is where **Quicken** comes in—a powerful and intuitive personal finance management tool designed to help individuals and families take full control of their financial well-being.

Quicken has been a trusted name in personal finance for decades, offering users a robust platform to track their spending, manage budgets, plan for the future, and gain clarity on their overall financial health. Whether you're a beginner looking for basic money management features or a seasoned user seeking advanced tools for investments and loans, Quicken provides an all-in-one solution tailored to your needs.

In this chapter, we will explore why Quicken is a game-changer in personal finance management. We'll discuss its key benefits, the importance of financial organization, and the features that make it an indispensable tool for individuals and families alike.

Understanding Quicken and Its Benefits

Quicken is more than just a financial tracking tool—it's a comprehensive financial management system that enables users to track their income, expenses, savings, debts, and investments in one place. Here are some of the core benefits of using Quicken:

- **Financial Clarity** – Quicken consolidates all your accounts, credit cards, loans, and investments in one dashboard, providing a clear picture of your financial health.

- **Automated Transactions** – You can sync your bank accounts with Quicken to automatically download transactions, categorize expenses, and eliminate manual data entry.

- **Budgeting and Goal Setting** – Create custom budgets, set savings goals, and track progress over time to ensure financial stability.

- **Bill and Payment Management** – Never miss a due date with Quicken's built-in bill reminder system, which helps you stay on top of payments.

- **Investment Tracking** – If you invest in stocks, bonds, or retirement accounts, Quicken offers tools to track performance and manage portfolios.

- **Debt Management** – Easily monitor loans, mortgages, and credit card debts with Quickens intuitive repayment features.

For those who struggle with keeping up with their finances, Quicken is a lifesaver that not only simplifies money management but also helps users build better financial habits.

The Importance of Personal Finance Management

Why is personal finance management so critical? Without a structured approach to tracking and managing money, individuals can find themselves living paycheck to paycheck, accumulating unnecessary debt, or failing to save for the future.

Proper personal finance management allows you to:

- **Plan for financial stability** by tracking income and expenses.

- **Avoid debt traps** by ensuring timely payments and responsible borrowing.

- **Achieve savings goals** by setting aside money for emergencies, vacations, or retirement.

- **Make informed investment decisions** by keeping track of assets and liabilities.

Using Quicken as your personal finance tool means gaining control over your money instead of letting money control you. It allows you to see exactly where your money is going and make strategic adjustments to improve financial health.

Key Features to Simplify Money Management

Quicken offers a **wide range of features** designed to cater to different financial needs. Here are some of the key tools that make managing money easier:

- **Account Synchronization** – Link bank accounts, credit cards, loans, and investments to track all finances in one place.

- **Expense Categorization** – Automatically categorizes transactions so you can see spending patterns.

- **Custom Budgeting Tools** – Create and manage personalized budgets to keep spending in check.

- **Debt Reduction Planning** – Calculate payoff strategies and interest savings for loans and credit cards.

- **Bill Reminders & Alerts** – Set up notifications to avoid missed payments.

- **Investment Monitoring** – Track stocks, bonds, and mutual funds with real-time updates.

By using these tools effectively, Quicken transforms financial management from a **tedious chore into an intuitive, streamlined process**.

CHAPTER 2

GETTING STARTED WITH QUICKEN

Now that we understand why Quicken is an essential tool for personal finance management, let's dive into the setup process. Setting up Quicken properly from the start will ensure you get the most out of its features while keeping your financial data accurate and organized.

This chapter will guide you through installing Quicken, setting up your account, navigating the dashboard, and managing transactions. By the end, you'll be ready to use Quicken confidently and efficiently.

Installing and Setting Up Quicken

Before you begin, you need to install Quicken on your device. Follow these steps:

1. **Download and Install** – Purchase and download Quicken from the official website. Run the installer and follow the on-screen instructions.

2. **Choose Your Version** – Quicken offers different versions (Starter, Deluxe, Premier, Home & Business) based on your needs.

3. **Create an Account** – Sign up for a Quicken account to access cloud syncing and updates.

4. **Enter Financial Information** – Add bank accounts, credit cards, loans, and investment accounts.

5. **Customize Settings** – Set preferences such as currency, backup frequency, and security options.

Once set up, you're ready to start managing your finances in Quicken.

Creating and Managing Your Quicken Account

Your Quicken account acts as the **central hub for your financial data**. Here's what you need to know:

- **Logging In and Security** – Use a strong password and enable multi-factor authentication for security.

- **Cloud Sync** – Enable cloud storage to access your finances from multiple devices.

- **Managing Multiple Accounts** – If you have separate finances (personal vs. business), Quicken allows you to track them separately.

Keeping your account updated and secure ensures smooth financial tracking.

Navigating the Quicken Dashboard

The **dashboard** is where you'll **monitor transactions, analyze spending trends, and plan budgets**. Key sections include:

- **Accounts Overview** – A snapshot of all linked bank and investment accounts.

- **Spending Graphs** – Visual breakdowns of expenses and income.

- **Bill Reminders** – Upcoming payment alerts to avoid late fees.

- **Budgeting Tools** – A customizable area for setting financial goals.

Familiarizing yourself with the dashboard makes daily financial tracking quick and effortless.

Manual Entry vs. Automatic Sync

You can enter transactions manually or use Quickens automatic sync feature:

- **Manual Entry** – Best for users who prefer full control over transaction details.

- **Automatic Sync** – Downloads transactions from linked accounts, reducing manual work.

Many users opt for a combination of both to ensure accuracy while minimizing effort.

Organizing Finances with Categories

Quicken allows you to categorize transactions for better financial insights:

- **Essentials** – Rent, groceries, utilities, transportation.

- **Discretionary** – Dining, shopping, entertainment.

- **Savings & Investments** – Retirement, emergency fund, stocks.

Proper categorization ensures realistic budgeting and better spending habits.

CHAPTER 3

MANAGING YOUR DAY-TO-DAY FINANCES

Money is a part of everyday life, yet managing it effectively remains a challenge for many. Whether you're tracking expenses, setting a budget, or planning for future financial goals, day-to-day money management is the foundation of financial stability and success. Without a clear plan, it's easy to overspend, accumulate debt, or feel overwhelmed by financial uncertainty. But the good news is that with the right tools and strategies, you can take control of your finances and achieve a sense of financial confidence.

Why Daily Money Management Matters

Many people think of financial planning as something reserved for big decisions—buying a house, saving for retirement, or investing in stocks. While long-term planning is important, the way you handle your everyday finances has a direct impact on your financial well-being. Small daily choices—whether it's making an impulse purchase, forgetting to pay a bill on time, or not tracking spending—can add up over time and lead to financial stress. On the other hand, developing smart money habits can create financial security, allowing you to save more, reduce debt, and prepare for unexpected expenses.

By actively managing your finances daily, you can:

- Avoid living paycheck to paycheck

- Reduce financial stress and anxiety

- Stay on top of bills and avoid late fees

- Improve savings and build an emergency fund

- Gain control over spending habits

- Work towards financial goals with confidence

The Role of Budgeting in Daily Finance Management

At the core of managing your day-to-day finances is **budgeting**—knowing exactly how much money is coming in, how much is going out, and where it's going. A well-structured budget helps you prioritize essential expenses like rent, groceries, and utilities while also allocating funds for savings, debt repayment, and personal spending.

Budgeting doesn't mean restricting yourself from things you enjoy—it's about making informed financial choices. With tools like **Quicken**, you can automate budgeting, track transactions, and categorize expenses effortlessly, making financial management more streamlined and less overwhelming.

Tracking and Organizing Expenses

One of the biggest challenges people faces is knowing where their money goes. Without tracking expenses, it's easy to underestimate spending and go over budget. Keeping track of daily expenses—whether through manual logs, spreadsheets, or financial software—allows you to identify spending patterns and make necessary adjustments.

Organizing your finances also means setting up systems for bill payments, subscriptions, and debt repayment. Late payments can lead to penalties and hurt your credit score, so automating bills or setting reminders can keep you on track. By staying organized, you eliminate financial guesswork and create a smoother financial routine.

Smart Spending and Saving Habits

A key aspect of day-to-day financial management is making intentional spending choices. Ask yourself:

- Do I really need this purchase, or is it a want?

- Is there a more cost-effective alternative?

- Can I wait before making this purchase?

Being mindful of your spending helps you avoid impulse buys and prioritize financial goals. Small savings on daily purchases—like making coffee at home instead of buying it every day—can add up significantly over time.

Additionally, establishing a habit of saving is crucial. Whether it's putting aside a small percentage of your income into an emergency fund or automatically transferring money to savings, consistent small actions lead to long-term financial stability.

Using Technology to Simplify Money Management

With advancements in financial technology, managing money is easier than ever. Tools like Quicken allow you to link bank accounts, track expenses, categorize transactions, and generate reports that provide a clear picture of your financial health. By leveraging technology, you reduce the time and effort needed for manual tracking and ensure better financial organization.

Taking Control of Your Financial Future

Managing your day-to-day finances isn't just about tracking numbers—it's about taking control of your financial future. By implementing simple habits like budgeting, tracking expenses, making mindful purchases, and using the right financial tools, you can reduce stress, improve savings, and work towards financial independence.

This book is designed to guide you through the essential aspects of financial management using Quicken and other effective strategies. Whether you're a beginner looking for financial clarity or someone aiming to refine your money management skills, this journey will help you build a strong financial foundation—one day at a time.

Tracking Income and Expenses

One of the most important steps in managing your day-to-day finances is keeping track of your income and expenses. Knowing how much money is coming in and where it's going ensures that you stay in control of your financial situation. Without a clear understanding of your cash flow, it's easy to overspend, miss bill payments, or fail to save for future needs. By tracking your income and expenses effectively, you can make informed financial decisions, avoid debt, and build a secure financial future.

Why Tracking Your Income Matters

Your income is the foundation of your financial plan. It includes all sources of money you receive, such as:

- Salary or wages from a job
- Side hustle earnings
- Freelance or contract payments

- Rental income

- Investments and dividends

- Government benefits or pensions

Understanding your total income helps you create a realistic budget and determine how much you can afford to spend and save each month. Many people only focus on their salary, but tracking all sources of income ensures that you maximize your financial potential.

Why Expense Tracking is Crucial

Your expenses represent where your money is going. If you don't monitor your spending habits, you may find yourself living paycheck to paycheck, struggling to save, or accumulating unnecessary debt. Tracking expenses allows you to:

- Identify unnecessary spending

- Cut back on non-essential purchases

- Avoid late fees and overdrafts

- Allocate funds wisely for savings and investment

- Maintain financial discipline and stability

Types of Expenses

Expenses generally fall into two categories:

1. **Fixed Expenses** – These are regular, consistent costs that don't change much from month to month, such as:

   o   Rent or mortgage payments

   o   Utilities (electricity, water, internet)

   o   Insurance (health, auto, home)

   o   Loan or credit card payments

   o   Subscription services (streaming platforms, gym memberships)

2. **Variable Expenses** – These fluctuate depending on your lifestyle and spending habits, including:

   o   Groceries

   o   Dining out and entertainment

   o   Shopping and personal expenses

   o   Transportation (fuel, ride-sharing, maintenance)

   o   Travel and leisure activities

Keeping an eye on both fixed and variable expenses helps you find opportunities to reduce unnecessary spending and adjust your budget when needed.

How to Track Your Income and Expenses

There are multiple ways to track income and expenses, ranging from simple pen-and-paper methods to advanced financial software. Here are some popular approaches:

1. Manual Tracking (Notebook or Spreadsheet)

If you prefer a hands-on approach, you can use a notebook or a spreadsheet to record every transaction. This method allows you to:

- Write down your income and expenses daily
- Categorize spending (groceries, utilities, transportation)
- Analyze patterns over time

Spreadsheets (such as Microsoft Excel or Google Sheets) allow for easy calculations and summaries, helping you visualize spending trends.

2. Budgeting Apps and Financial Software

Tools like Quicken, Mint, and YNAB (You Need a Budget) automate expense tracking by linking to your bank accounts, credit cards, and investment portfolios. These apps can:

- Automatically categorize transactions
- Provide real-time spending insights
- Generate detailed financial reports

- Set reminders for bill payments

Using budgeting software simplifies money management and reduces the risk of human error.

3. Envelope System (Cash-Based Tracking)

If you prefer using cash, the envelope system is an effective way to control spending. You allocate cash into envelopes labeled for different expenses, such as groceries, dining, and gas, and only spend what's inside each envelope. Once the cash is gone, you stop spending in that category until the next budget cycle.

4. Bank and Credit Card Statements

Reviewing bank statements and credit card transactions regularly can help you track where your money is going. Many banks provide spending breakdowns, helping you identify excessive spending in certain categories.

The Importance of Reviewing Your Finances Regularly

Tracking income and expenses isn't a one-time task—it requires ongoing monitoring and adjustments. At the end of each week or month, review your spending habits and ask yourself:

- Am I sticking to my budget?

- Are there any unnecessary expenses I can cut?

- Do I need to adjust my savings goals?

By consistently tracking your income and expenses, you gain financial clarity, reduce stress, and set yourself up for long-term financial success. Whether you use a simple notebook, a spreadsheet, or an advanced tool like **Quicken**, staying aware of your financial inflows and outflows is the key to building a strong financial future.

Building and Maintaining a Budget

A well-structured budget is the foundation of financial stability. It helps you control spending, save effectively, and achieve financial goals without unnecessary stress. Budgeting is not about restriction—it is about allocating your money wisely so you can cover essentials, enjoy life, and plan for the future. Whether you are trying to pay off debt, save for a big purchase, or simply gain better control over your finances, building and maintaining a budget is a crucial step.

Why Budgeting Matters

A budget allows you to:

- Track your income and expenses to ensure you are living within your means

- Avoid unnecessary debt by ensuring you are not spending more than you earn

- Set and achieve financial goals, such as saving for a home, emergency fund, or retirement

- Reduce financial stress by eliminating uncertainty about your financial standing

- Prepare for unexpected expenses without derailing your finances

Steps to Building a Budget

1. Determine Your Total Income

The first step in creating a budget is understanding how much money you have coming in. Your income sources may include:

- Salary or wages

- Freelance or side hustle earnings

- Rental income

- Investment returns

- Government benefits or pensions

When budgeting, **focus on your net income** (the amount you take home after taxes and deductions) rather than your gross income. This gives you a **realistic picture** of what you can actually spend.

2. List and Categorize Your Expenses

Once you have identified your income, track your expenses. These generally fall into two categories:

- **Fixed Expenses** – These remain consistent every month, such as:

  - Rent or mortgage payments

  - Insurance (health, car, home)

  - Loan or credit card payments

  - Internet, phone, and utilities

  - Subscription services (streaming platforms, gym memberships)

- **Variable Expenses** – This change based on your lifestyle and spending habits, including:

  - Groceries and dining out

  - Entertainment and shopping

  - Transportation (gas, maintenance, public transit)

  - Travel and leisure

  - Miscellaneous or discretionary spending

A clear understanding of both fixed and variable expenses helps you identify areas where you can cut back and allocate funds more efficiently.

3. Set Spending Limits and Prioritize Essential Costs

Once you know your income and expenses, establish spending limits for each category. The goal is to allocate funds efficiently while ensuring you are not spending beyond your means.

A popular budgeting rule is the 50/30/20 method, which divides income into:

- 50% for necessities (housing, utilities, insurance, food)

- 30% for wants (entertainment, dining, vacations)

- 20% for savings and debt repayment

Adjust these percentages based on your financial goals and lifestyle.

4. Allocate Money for Savings and Emergencies

A budget should always include a savings plan. Some key savings categories include:

- **Emergency Fund:** Covers unexpected expenses such as medical bills, car repairs, or job loss. Aim for at least three to six months' worth of expenses.

- **Retirement Savings:** Contributing to a 401(k), IRA, or other retirement accounts ensures long-term financial security.

- **Short-Term and Long-Term Goals:** Whether it's a vacation, home purchase, or education fund, setting aside money consistently will help you reach your goals.

5. Track Your Spending and Adjust as Needed

A budget is not a one-time plan—it requires regular tracking and adjustments. You can use:

- Manual tracking with a notebook or spreadsheet

- Budgeting apps and financial tools like Quicken, Mint, or YNAB (You Need a Budget)

- Bank and credit card statements to analyze spending trends

Review your budget weekly or monthly to check for areas where you are overspending and make necessary changes.

Maintaining a Budget for Long-Term Success

1. Automate Savings and Bill Payments

Set up automatic transfers to your savings and investment accounts to ensure consistency. Automate bill payments to avoid late fees and maintain a good credit score.

2. Identify and Cut Unnecessary Expenses

Regularly evaluate your spending habits. Some simple ways to cut back on non-essential expenses include:

- Cooking at home instead of eating out

- Cancelling unused subscriptions

- Shopping with a list to avoid impulse purchases

- Using public transportation or carpooling

-

3. Adjust Your Budget as Your Financial Situation Changes

Your financial situation will change over time due to job shifts, life events, or unexpected expenses. Periodically review your budget to ensure it aligns with your current financial priorities and goals.

4. Stay Motivated and Set Rewards

Sticking to a budget can be challenging, but setting small financial milestones and rewarding yourself for reaching them can keep you motivated. For example, if you hit a savings goal, treat yourself to something small and affordable.

Building and maintaining a budget is the key to financial stability and long-term success. By tracking your income, controlling expenses, and prioritizing savings, you can achieve your financial goals while avoiding unnecessary debt and financial stress. Whether you use a simple spreadsheet or advanced budgeting software like Quicken, a well-maintained budget will keep your finances on track and help you build a secure financial future.

Managing Bills, Payments, and Reminders

Staying on top of your bills and payments is essential for maintaining financial stability and avoiding unnecessary fees, penalties, or damage to your credit score. A well-organized bill management system ensures that you never miss a payment, keep track of due dates, and avoid late fees or service interruptions.

With the right approach, you can simplify the process of handling bills, automate payments, and set up reminders to make financial management stress-free.

Why Effective Bill Management Matters

Failing to manage your bills properly can lead to:

- Late fees and penalties

- Increased interest rates on loans or credit cards

- Service disruptions (electricity, water, internet, phone, etc.)

- A negative impact on your credit score

On the other hand, staying organized with payments can help you:

- Maintain a good credit history

- Reduce financial stress

- Avoid unnecessary financial setbacks

- Free up more time by automating the process

Steps to Efficiently Manage Bills and Payments

1. Keep a List of All Bills and Due Dates

The first step in managing your bills is to identify all recurring payments and their due dates. This includes:

- Fixed bills (rent/mortgage, insurance, loan payments)

- Variable bills (utilities, credit cards, phone bills)

- Subscription services (streaming platforms, memberships)

- Annual or semi-annual payments (property taxes, vehicle registration, insurance premiums)

Create a bill tracking system using a spreadsheet, notebook, or financial app to keep everything in one place.

2. Automate Payments Whenever Possible

Many banks and service providers offer autopay options, allowing you to set up automatic withdrawals for recurring bills. This ensures you never miss a due date and eliminates the risk of late fees.

When setting up automatic payments:

- Ensure sufficient funds are in your bank account to avoid overdraft fees.

- Set up autopay for fixed expenses first (mortgage, insurance, loan payments).

- For variable bills, review each statement before autopay is processed to catch errors or unexpected charges.

3. Use Payment Reminders

If you prefer to pay bills manually or have bills that fluctuate each month, setting reminders is crucial. You can:

- Use calendar alerts on your phone or computer.

- Set up text or email notifications from your bank or service providers.

- Use bill reminder apps like Quicken, Mint, or YNAB (You Need a Budget).

4. Prioritize Essential Payments First

When money is tight, always prioritize the most important bills first:

- Housing costs (rent/mortgage)

- Utilities (electricity, water, gas)

- Loan and credit card payments (to avoid interest accumulation)

- Insurance (health, car, home)

If you're struggling financially, consider negotiating with service providers for lower payments, temporary relief, or extended due dates.

5. Organize and Store Payment Records

Keeping records of your payments is essential for tracking expenses, disputing incorrect charges, and budgeting effectively. Save copies of bills, bank statements, and receipts either digitally or in a dedicated folder.

Some useful ways to store records include:

- Cloud storage (Google Drive, Dropbox)

- Expense tracking apps

- A dedicated finance notebook or binder

6. Review and Adjust Your Payment Strategy Regularly

Bills and payment amounts may change over time due to rate adjustments, new expenses, or changes in income. Review your financial commitments monthly to:

- Ensure all payments are made on time.

- Identify any unnecessary expenses that can be reduced or eliminated.

- Adjust your budget if necessary to accommodate financial changes.

Tips for Avoiding Late Payments

- **Schedule payments in advance** to avoid last-minute issues.

- **Align due dates with your payday** so funds are always available.

- **Use bill-pay features** offered by banks or financial software.

- **Negotiate with providers** for better rates or extended due dates if needed.

Managing bills, payments, and reminders efficiently is key to maintaining a healthy financial life. With a structured approach—such as automating payments, tracking due dates, and setting up reminders—you can avoid stress, save time, and ensure your financial obligations are met without difficulty. By staying proactive, you create financial stability and peace of mind, allowing you to focus on other important aspects of your life.

Handling Debts and Loans Efficiently

Managing debt and loans effectively is a critical aspect of maintaining a healthy financial life. Whether it's credit card debt, student loans, a mortgage, or personal loans, managing these financial obligations responsibly can help you avoid overwhelming interest charges, stress, and long-term financial struggles. The goal is to handle debts and loans in a way that minimizes financial strain, helps you pay them off faster, and ultimately puts you on a path to greater financial freedom.

Why Efficient Debt Management Matters

Debt management is essential for several reasons:

- **Maintaining a good credit score**: Your ability to pay off loans on time directly impacts your credit rating, which affects your borrowing ability in the future.

- **Reducing stress**: Carrying debt without a plan can be stressful. By managing it efficiently, you can reduce anxiety about money.

- **Saving money on interest**: By paying off loans early or on time, you can reduce the amount you pay in interest, saving money in the long term.

- **Financial freedom**: Reducing debt allows you to redirect funds toward savings, investments, or other important financial goals.

Steps to Handling Debt and Loans Efficiently

1. Know Your Debt and Loan Details

The first step in managing your debts and loans is understanding the specifics of each one:

- **Loan Type**: What kind of loans do you have? This could include credit card debt, student loans, personal loans, mortgages, etc.

- **Interest Rates**: Different loans have different interest rates, which affect how much you'll pay over time. Higher interest rates mean higher payments and more money paid in interest.

- **Minimum Payments**: Always know the minimum payment required for each debt. Missing or underpaying can lead to penalties and additional interest charges.

- **Due Dates**: Keep track of when payments are due. Missing due dates can harm your credit score and lead to additional fees.

Create a **list or spreadsheet** that outlines the type of debt, interest rates, minimum payments, and due dates for all of your loans. This will help you gain a clear picture of your obligations and plan your payments accordingly.

2. Prioritize Debts Based on Interest Rates

Not all debts are created equal. Some loans have higher interest rates than others, meaning they will cost you more over time. To pay off debts efficiently:

- **Pay off high-interest debts first**: Focus on eliminating debts with the highest interest rates (typically credit card debt). This strategy is known as the **debt avalanche method**.

- **Pay the minimum on other debts**: While focusing on the high-interest debt, continue making the minimum payments on other loans to avoid penalties.

Alternatively, some people prefer the **debt snowball method**, which involves paying off the smallest debt first to build momentum. However, the avalanche method is often more cost-effective in the long run.

3. Create a Repayment Plan

Once you understand your debts and have prioritized them, it's time to create a repayment plan. There are two common strategies:

- **Debt Avalanche**: Focus extra payments on the highest-interest debt first. Once it's paid off, move to the next highest interest rate debt.

- **Debt Snowball**: Pay off the smallest debt first, then move on to the next smallest. This can provide a psychological boost as you see your debts disappear.

Regardless of the method you choose, ensure that you are **consistent with your payments** and avoid taking on additional debt while working to pay down existing obligations.

4. Consider Debt Consolidation or Refinancing

If you have multiple loans or high-interest credit card debt, debt consolidation or refinancing may be an option. These strategies can:

- **Simplify payments**: Instead of juggling multiple payments, consolidation combines your debts into one loan, typically with a lower interest rate.

- **Lower interest rates**: Refinancing involves taking out a new loan to pay off existing debt, potentially at a lower interest rate.

Be mindful that debt consolidation or refinancing may come with fees or longer repayment terms, so weigh the pros and cons before proceeding.

5. Negotiate With Creditors or Lenders

If you're struggling to make payments, don't hesitate to reach out to your creditors or lenders. In many cases, they may be willing to work with you to create a more manageable payment plan. Possible solutions include:

- **Lowering interest rates**: Some lenders may reduce your interest rate if you're having trouble keeping up with payments.

- **Deferred payments**: Some lenders allow you to defer payments for a short period during financial hardship (often with interest still accumulating).

- **Flexible repayment terms**: Lenders may offer extended terms, allowing you to lower monthly payments.

6. Avoid Accumulating More Debt

While you're working to manage existing debts, it's crucial to **avoid adding more debt**. Consider these tips:

- **Cut unnecessary expenses**: Trim your discretionary spending to free up money for debt repayment.

- **Stop using credit cards**: Leave your credit cards at home or cut them up if necessary to prevent additional charges.

- **Live within your means**: Focus on budgeting and living within your income to avoid borrowing more.

7. Consider Seeking Professional Help

If you're feeling overwhelmed by debt, seeking the help of a professional can be a smart move. Options include:

- **Credit counseling**: Nonprofit credit counseling agencies can help you create a debt management plan and negotiate with creditors on your behalf.

- **Debt management programs (DMPs)**: These programs consolidate your debts into a single payment, and credit counselors may negotiate lower interest rates with creditors.

- **Debt settlement**: In more extreme cases, debt settlement services negotiate with creditors to settle your debts for less than you owe, but this option can have long-term impacts on your credit score.

Efficiently handling debts and loans is crucial for achieving financial stability. By understanding your debt, prioritizing high-interest loans, creating a solid repayment plan, and considering consolidation or refinancing options, you can **take control of your financial future**. With consistency and discipline, you can pay off debt faster, reduce financial stress, and ultimately achieve a debt-free life, setting the stage for greater financial freedom and security.

CHAPTER 4

ADVANCED FEATURES FOR EXPERIENCED USERS

Once you've mastered the basics of financial management and are comfortable with tracking your income, expenses, and budgeting, it's time to take your financial skills to the next level. Advanced features can help you gain deeper insights into your financial situation, automate complex tasks, and optimize your strategies for greater efficiency and control.

For experienced users, the goal is not just about managing daily transactions but about leveraging sophisticated tools and techniques to fine-tune your financial approach, improve decision-making, and ultimately reach your long-term financial goals. Whether it's using advanced budgeting techniques, automating investment tracking, or analyzing data to identify trends, these features will give you a more powerful and proactive way to manage your finances.

This section will explore some of the most effective advanced features available to users who are ready to take their financial management to the next level. From advanced investment tracking to using financial software for more detailed budgeting, we'll dive into the tools and strategies that will enhance your ability to manage and grow your wealth with precision and insight.

Tracking and Managing Investments

Effectively tracking and managing investments is a key part of building long-term wealth and achieving financial goals. As your investment portfolio grows, it becomes increasingly important to monitor its performance, diversify your assets, and make informed decisions about where to allocate your funds. By staying organized and proactive, you can optimize returns, minimize risk, and ensure that your investments align with your financial objectives.

Why Tracking Investments is Important

Investments, whether in stocks, bonds, mutual funds, or real estate, require ongoing monitoring to:

- **Evaluate performance**: Regularly reviewing your investments helps you identify trends, assess returns, and adjust your strategy as needed.

- **Manage risk**: Understanding your portfolio's risk exposure allows you to make adjustments, like diversifying or reallocating funds, to protect against market volatility.

- **Optimize returns**: Monitoring helps you spot opportunities to buy, sell, or adjust your investments to improve returns over time.

- **Stay aligned with goals**: Regular tracking ensures that your investment strategy stays in line with your financial goals, whether they involve retirement, saving for a home, or funding education.

Steps to Effectively Track and Manage Investments

1. Create a Comprehensive Investment Portfolio

Start by organizing your investments in one place. This could be done manually in a spreadsheet, or through financial software or apps that allow you to track multiple investment types. Your portfolio should include:

- Stock investments (individual stocks or exchange-traded funds – ETFs)

- Bonds (corporate, municipal, or government bonds)

- Mutual funds (actively or passively managed funds)

- Real estate investments (properties, REITs, etc.)

- Other alternative assets (cryptocurrencies, collectibles, etc.)

Ensure that each investment includes key details such as purchase price, current value, dividends, yields, and any associated fees or expenses.

2. Monitor Performance Regularly

To track the performance of your investments, you should:

- **Review returns**: Check the growth or loss of each asset over specific periods, such as monthly, quarterly, or annually. This allows you to spot trends and determine whether an investment is performing as expected.

- **Benchmark performance**: Compare your portfolio's returns against relevant benchmarks (e.g., market indexes like the S&P 500) to gauge whether you're outperforming or underperforming.

- **Track dividends and interest**: Keep an eye on passive income generated from investments, such as dividends from stocks or interest from bonds.

Using financial apps like Quicken, Mint, or Personal Capital can help you track performance in real-time and provide easy-to-understand reports.

3. Diversify Your Portfolio

Diversification helps spread risk across various asset classes, reducing the impact of poor performance in any one investment. A well-diversified portfolio typically includes:

- **Stocks** (individual shares, mutual funds, ETFs)

- **Bonds** (government, municipal, corporate)

- **Real estate** (rental properties, REITs)

- **Commodities** (gold, oil, agricultural products)

- **Cash equivalents** (money market funds, CDs)

By investing across different asset types, industries, and geographical locations, you can reduce the overall risk of your portfolio while maximizing potential returns.

4. Rebalance Your Portfolio

Over time, some investments will grow faster than others, and your portfolio may become unbalanced. Rebalancing involves adjusting the allocation of assets to maintain your desired level of risk and return. This might include:

- **Selling investments** that have grown disproportionately, such as stocks or bonds that no longer fit within your target allocation.

- **Buying more of underperforming investments** or areas that need more exposure to stay in line with your overall financial goals.

Rebalancing is typically done on a regular schedule (annually, semi-annually) or when significant changes in the market or your personal circumstances occur.

5. Set Goals and Track Progress

Clearly define your financial goals, such as saving for retirement, purchasing a home, or funding education. With each goal, determine:

- **The amount of money needed**: How much do you need to reach your goal?

- **The time frame**: When do you want to achieve this goal?

- **The type of investments**: What kind of assets will help you reach that goal (stocks, bonds, real estate, etc.)?

Tracking your investment progress toward these goals will help you stay motivated and make necessary adjustments to your strategy.

6. Leverage Tax-Advantaged Accounts

To optimize your returns, consider utilizing **tax-advantaged accounts** such as:

- **IRAs** (Individual Retirement Accounts): These offer tax benefits for retirement savings.

- **401(k) or 403(b)**: Employer-sponsored retirement accounts with potential for matching contributions.

- **HSAs** (Health Savings Accounts): Useful for covering medical expenses while also offering tax advantages.

These accounts help reduce your taxable income while allowing your investments to grow tax-deferred or tax-free, depending on the type of account.

7. Stay Informed and Educated

To make informed investment decisions, keep up with market news, trends, and economic changes. Staying educated on financial topics, market conditions, and investment strategies will help you make proactive decisions about your portfolio.

Consider following:

- **Financial news websites** (e.g., Bloomberg, Reuters)

- **Investment blogs and podcasts**

- **Books and courses** on investing strategies

Additionally, periodically review your investment strategy and adjust it based on market conditions or changes in your personal financial situation.

8. Use Technology for Investment Management

Technology has made managing investments easier than ever. There are several tools available to help you:

- **Robo-advisors**: These automated platforms use algorithms to create and manage a diversified portfolio based on your risk tolerance and goals.

- **Investment tracking software**: Platforms like **Quicken, Personal Capital, or Morningstar** can help track performance, calculate returns, and analyze your portfolio.

- **Stock screeners**: These tools allow you to search for stocks or funds based on specific criteria, such as industry, market cap, or dividend yield.

These tools not only simplify investment management but also provide real-time insights and help automate the process of tracking and rebalancing your portfolio.

Tracking and managing investments effectively requires attention to detail, a solid strategy, and the use of the right tools. By regularly monitoring performance, diversifying your portfolio, and making informed decisions, you can optimize your investments to align with your long-term financial goals. With these practices in place, you can confidently build a well-rounded portfolio that supports your wealth-building journey and ensures financial security for the future.

Generating and Customizing Financial Reports

Generating and customizing financial reports is an essential part of managing your finances, whether for personal use or business purposes. These reports provide a clear and organized view of your financial health, allowing you to analyze income, expenses, and investments while making informed decisions for future planning. By leveraging financial reporting tools and customizing them to your needs, you can gain better insights into your financial situation and track your progress towards achieving your financial goals.

Why Financial Reports Matter

Financial reports are invaluable for:

- **Tracking progress**: Reports help you visualize your financial journey by showcasing trends in income, expenses, savings, and investments.

- **Identifying patterns**: By reviewing reports regularly, you can spot areas where you're overspending, areas to save, or where your investments are performing well.

- **Tax filing**: Financial reports help prepare for tax season by categorizing income and deductible expenses, simplifying the tax preparation process.

- **Making informed decisions**: Well-organized reports allow you to make data-driven decisions, whether it's adjusting your budget, rebalancing investments, or planning for the future.

- **Budgeting**: Reports can highlight discrepancies in your spending, which is useful when evaluating the effectiveness of your budget and making adjustments.

Types of Financial Reports

There are various financial reports you can generate, each serving a different purpose:

1. Income Statement (Profit and Loss Statement)

An income statement provides a detailed overview of your revenue and expenses over a set period, typically monthly or annually. This report allows you to assess:

- **Total income**: The money you earned over the period.

- **Total expenses**: Your costs, including fixed (e.g., rent, utilities) and variable (e.g., groceries, entertainment).

- **Net income**: The difference between income and expenses, showing whether you made a profit or a loss during that period.

2. Balance Sheet

A balance sheet provides a snapshot of your financial position at a specific point in time. It lists:

- **Assets**: What you own (e.g., cash, property, investments).

- **Liabilities**: What you owe (e.g., debts, loans, bills).

- **Equity**: The difference between your assets and liabilities, representing your net worth.

This report is essential for evaluating your overall financial stability and determining how much you owe versus how much you own.

3. Cash Flow Statement

The cash flow statement tracks the movement of money in and out of your finances. It is essential for understanding:

- **Cash inflows**: Income from salary, business revenue, investments, etc.

- **Cash outflows**: Payments for expenses, loans, and other liabilities.

- **Net cash flow**: The difference between cash inflows and outflows, indicating whether you're generating more money than you're spending.

By tracking your cash flow, you can ensure you have enough liquidity to meet obligations and avoid cash shortages.

4. Budget vs. Actual Report

This report compares your planned budget with actual spending, allowing you to see how closely you are sticking to your financial goals. It helps in identifying:

- **Areas of overspending**: Where your actual expenses exceeded your budget.

- **Underutilized budget categories**: Areas where you have money left over, which can be redirected to other priorities.

This report is crucial for adjusting your financial habits and staying on track with your budgeting.

5. Investment Portfolio Report

If you're managing investments, an investment portfolio report provides a breakdown of your investments and their performance. This includes:

- **Asset allocation**: The percentage of your portfolio invested in different asset classes (stocks, bonds, real estate, etc.).

- **Returns**: The gains or losses on each investment.

- **Dividends**: Earnings from investments that generate income.

This report helps track the success of your investment strategy and informs decisions on buying, selling, or reallocating investments.

How to Generate Financial Reports

Most financial software, such as **Quicken**, **Mint**, or **QuickBooks**, offers built-in tools for generating reports. Here's how to generate and customize your reports:

1. Select Your Financial Tool

Choose a tool that suits your financial needs, whether it's for personal budgeting or business accounting. Some popular tools include:

- **Quicken**: Ideal for personal finance management, offering detailed reports on income, expenses, investments, and budgeting.

- **QuickBooks**: Excellent for small business owners, providing in-depth reports on revenue, expenses, taxes, and cash flow.

- **Mint**: A user-friendly tool that tracks spending, generates reports, and offers budgeting assistance.

2. Set the Time Frame

Choose the period for which you want to generate reports. This could be:

- **Monthly**: Ideal for tracking short-term financial activities like monthly expenses or income.

- **Quarterly**: Useful for reviewing trends over three months.

- **Annually**: Best for big-picture analysis, such as evaluating your overall financial health, tax planning, and long-term goals.

3. Customize the Report Categories

Depending on the software, you can tailor the categories that appear in your financial report. Customize reports to reflect specific types of income, expenses, or investments that are most relevant to your goals. For example:

- **Track certain expense categories** like groceries, utilities, entertainment, etc.

- **Include specific investment types**, such as stocks, bonds, or mutual funds.

- **Filter reports by account types**, such as checking, savings, or credit cards.

4. Review and Interpret Your Report

Once the report is generated, take the time to analyze it:

- **Look for patterns** in your spending and income.

- **Assess performance** in investments and compare it to benchmarks.

- **Compare your actual spending** against your budget and identify areas to improve.

5. Adjust and Take Action

Use the insights gained from the report to make informed financial decisions. Whether it's rebalancing your investment portfolio, cutting down on unnecessary expenses, or adjusting your budget, the goal is to continuously improve your financial strategy.

Customizing Your Reports

To get the most value from your financial reports, it's important to customize them to your specific needs. Here are some customization tips:

- **Group categories**: If you have various income or expense types, group them into broader categories for easier analysis. For example, group all entertainment expenses under one category rather than listing each individual expense.

- **Use filters**: Apply filters to focus on specific accounts, time periods, or financial categories that matter most.

- **Create custom templates**: Many tools allow you to create your own templates for recurring reports, saving you time on future reports.

- **Export and share**: Most financial tools allow you to export reports as PDFs or Excel files for easy sharing with financial advisors, accountants, or other relevant parties.

Generating and customizing financial reports is essential for maintaining control over your finances. These reports provide a clear and organized view of your financial health, helping you make informed decisions about budgeting, investments, and overall financial strategy. By regularly reviewing and customizing your reports, you can stay on top of your financial goals and ensure you're always moving in the right direction.

Tax Planning Made Simple

Tax planning is an essential aspect of managing your finances, ensuring that you are not only compliant with the law but also minimizing your tax liability in the most effective way possible. While taxes can feel overwhelming, proper tax planning can make the process straightforward and even help you retain more of your hard-earned income. Understanding the key principles and strategies can take the stress out of tax season and leave you feeling confident about your financial decisions.

Why Tax Planning is Important

Tax planning allows you to:

- **Minimize your tax liability**: By strategically planning your income, deductions, and credits, you can reduce the amount of taxes you owe, keeping more of your money.

- **Stay compliant**: Proper tax planning ensures you meet all the legal requirements, preventing penalties and fines from incorrect or late filings.

- **Optimize your financial goals**: With an effective tax strategy, you can better allocate funds towards savings, investments, and other financial goals, ensuring that taxes do not hinder your financial growth.

- **Maximize tax credits and deductions**: Tax planning helps you identify opportunities to lower your taxable income through eligible deductions and credits, such as for mortgage interest, medical expenses, or education costs.

Key Concepts in Tax Planning

Understanding the following key concepts will simplify your tax planning process:

1. Taxable Income

Taxable income is the amount of your income that is subject to tax, after accounting for deductions and exemptions. It includes your wages, salary, rental income, dividends, and more. The more you can reduce your taxable income through deductions, the less you'll owe in taxes.

2. Deductions and Credits

- **Deductions**: These are expenses that reduce your taxable income. Common deductions include mortgage interest, student loan interest, medical expenses, charitable donations, and business expenses (for self-employed individuals).

- **Credits**: Tax credits directly reduce the amount of tax you owe. For example, education credits or earned income tax credits can significantly reduce your final tax bill.

3. Tax Brackets

Income tax is progressive, meaning the more you earn, the higher the percentage of your income you pay in taxes. Tax brackets define how much tax you owe at different levels of income. A well-crafted tax plan can help ensure you don't move into a higher tax bracket unnecessarily.

4. Filing Status

Your filing status (e.g., single, married filing jointly, head of household) plays a significant role in determining your tax rates and eligibility for certain deductions and credits. It's important to choose the status that works best for your situation to optimize your tax savings.

Basic Tax Planning Strategies

Here are some simple yet effective strategies to help you plan your taxes and reduce your overall tax burden:

1. Contribute to Tax-Advantaged Accounts

One of the easiest ways to reduce taxable income is by contributing to tax-advantaged accounts like:

- **401(k) or IRA (Individual Retirement Account)**: Contributions to these retirement accounts can reduce your taxable income for the year. Additionally, the growth of these investments is tax-deferred, meaning you won't pay taxes on the earnings until retirement.

- **Health Savings Account (HSA)**: Contributions to an HSA are tax-deductible, and withdrawals for qualified medical expenses are tax-free.

- **Flexible Spending Account (FSA)**: FSAs allow you to set aside pre-tax dollars for medical expenses or dependent care, reducing your taxable income.

2. Take Advantage of Tax Credits

Tax credits are more valuable than deductions because they directly reduce your tax liability. Some common credits include:

- **Child Tax Credit**: If you have dependent children, you may be eligible for a credit to reduce your tax bill.

- **Education Credits**: Credits like the American Opportunity Tax Credit (AOTC) and Lifetime Learning Credit (LLC) can help offset the cost of higher education expenses.

- **Earned Income Tax Credit (EITC)**: This is a credit designed to help lower-income workers, potentially providing a substantial refund.

3. Maximize Deductions

- **Itemize Deductions**: While the standard deduction is simple, itemizing deductions can lead to greater tax savings if you have significant expenses, such as mortgage interest, medical costs, or charitable donations.

- **Business Deductions**: If you're self-employed, you can deduct business-related expenses like office supplies, travel, and home office costs.

4. Timing Income and Expenses

Timing is crucial in tax planning. If you can control when income is received or expenses are paid, it may make sense to defer income or accelerate expenses to reduce taxable income in the current year. For example:

- **Deferring Income**: If you expect to be in a lower tax bracket in the following year, you might want to defer some income, like a bonus, until next year.

- **Accelerating Expenses**: If you're expecting a higher income next year, you could accelerate some deductible expenses into the current year, such as paying bills or making charitable donations early.

5. Plan for Capital Gains and Losses

If you have investments, it's important to manage your capital gains and losses efficiently. Capital gains occur when you sell an asset, such as stocks, for more than you paid for it. Managing when to sell investments and how to offset gains with losses (tax-loss harvesting) can reduce your tax bill.

6. Stay Organized Throughout the Year

One of the most important steps in tax planning is staying organized. Keep track of all income sources, deductions, and credits throughout the year. Set aside time each quarter to review your finances and estimate your tax liability. This will help you avoid surprises come tax season and give you time to make necessary adjustments.

Using Tax Software for Simple Planning

Today, there are many user-friendly tax software options available to help with tax planning, including **Quicken**, **TurboTax**, and **H&R Block**. These tools allow you to easily track income, expenses, and deductions and provide personalized recommendations for tax-saving strategies. They can also help you calculate estimated taxes throughout the year, making it easier to plan ahead.

Tax planning doesn't have to be complicated. With a basic understanding of the key concepts and strategies, you can take control of your taxes and minimize your liability. By staying organized, contributing to tax-advantaged accounts, maximizing deductions and credits, and using tools like tax software, you can ensure that tax season is stress-free and that you're keeping as much of your money as possible. Whether you're an individual or a business owner, tax planning is an essential skill for securing your financial future.

Personalizing Categories and Tags

Personalizing categories and tags is a powerful way to stay organized and streamline your financial tracking. In software like Quicken, categories and tags are essential tools that allow you to sort, track, and analyze your financial transactions more effectively. By customizing these features, you can create a system that suits your specific needs and goals, making it easier to monitor your income, expenses, investments, and savings.

What are Categories and Tags?

- **Categories**: These are broad classifications that group similar transactions together. For example, you might have categories for "Groceries," "Utilities," "Entertainment," or "Mortgage." Categories provide a general overview of your spending habits, helping you identify where your money is going each month.

- **Tags**: Tags are more specific labels you can assign to individual transactions within a category. They allow for a finer level of detail and can be used to track special projects, events, or specific types of purchases. For instance, you could use tags like "Vacation," "Holiday Shopping," or "Home Renovation" to track specific expenses that fall under a broader category, such as "Travel" or "Home Improvement."

Personalizing these elements enables you to have better control over your financial data, providing insights tailored to your unique circumstances.

Why Personalize Categories and Tags?

1. **Improve Financial Tracking**: By customizing your categories and tags, you create a financial tracking system that mirrors your lifestyle and spending habits. This allows for more accurate reports, helping you stay on top of your budget and savings goals.

2. **Gain Deeper Insights**: Personalized categories and tags allow you to break down your spending in ways that go beyond simple budgeting. For example, you can track how much you spend on eating out, subscriptions, or specific projects. This insight helps you identify areas where you can cut back or where you're overspending.

3. **Simplify Tax Filing**: Personalized tags can help you categorize transactions that are tax-deductible, making tax season easier and less stressful. For example, using tags like "Medical Expenses," "Charitable Donations," or "Business Expenses" ensures that you can quickly identify deductible expenses at the end of the year.

4. **Align with Financial Goals**: If you have specific financial goals like saving for a house, paying off debt, or building an emergency fund, personalizing categories and tags helps you track how much you're allocating toward those goals each month. You can create tags like "House Fund" or "Debt Repayment" to help monitor your progress.

How to Personalize Categories and Tags in Quicken

1. Create Custom Categories

While Quicken comes with a set of default categories, creating custom ones allows you to better match your needs. Here's how you can do it:

- Go to the **Categories List** in Quicken.

- Click on **Add Category** to create a new one. You can name it anything you like, such as "Vacation," "Business Expenses," or "Family Savings."

- Assign the category to transactions as they occur, helping you track those expenses accurately.

To make the categories more effective:

- **Assign Subcategories**: For instance, under "Groceries," you could create subcategories like "Organic," "Discount," or "Bulk Purchases" to break down your spending further.

- **Review and Update Regularly**: As your financial situation evolves, periodically review your categories to ensure they still align with your current lifestyle and goals.

2. Add Custom Tags

Tags in Quicken are particularly useful for adding extra details to your transactions. To add or personalize tags:

- When entering a transaction, you can choose to add a tag in the transaction window.

- Create tags like "Business Trip," "Vacation Fund," "Gifts," or any other tag that reflects the nature of the purchase.

- You can apply multiple tags to a single transaction if it falls under more than one category. For example, a dinner bill during a business trip could be tagged with both "Business Trip" and "Dining Out."

3. Use Tags for Event or Project Tracking

If you're managing a large project or a special event, tags can help keep things organized. For example, if you're planning a wedding, you could create tags like "Wedding Dress," "Venue," and "Catering." You can then see the total amount spent on each aspect of the event and track how well you're staying within your budget.

4. Set Up Automated Rules

Quicken allows you to automate the categorization process by setting up rules. If you frequently make similar purchases (e.g., grocery store visits, monthly utilities), you can create rules to automatically categorize those expenses as they appear in your transactions. This saves time and ensures consistency in your tracking.

5. Reporting with Categories and Tags

Once your categories and tags are personalized, you can generate financial reports based on them. Quicken allows you to create detailed reports that show how much you're spending in each category or on specific tags. You can even compare spending across different months or categories to identify trends. Reports like:

- **Spending Summary**: Shows how much you spent by category over a specific period.

- **Budget vs. Actuals**: Compares your planned budget to actual spending in personalized categories.

Tips for Effective Personalization

- **Keep It Simple**: Avoid creating too many categories or tags, as this can make tracking more complicated. Focus on the key areas that are important to you.

- **Be Consistent**: Ensure that you consistently use your personalized categories and tags for every transaction. This consistency will make it easier to analyze your spending.

- **Update as Needed**: As your financial situation changes, don't hesitate to update your categories and tags to reflect your new goals or lifestyle.

Personalizing categories and tags in Quicken can provide a more organized, insightful, and tailored approach to managing your finances. By creating a system that reflects your unique spending habits and financial goals, you can gain a deeper understanding of where your money goes and make smarter financial decisions. With personalized categories and tags, you'll have more control over your finances, making it easier to stay on track with your budget, savings goals, and long-term financial plans.

CHAPTER 5

OPTIMIZING YOUR FINANCIAL STRATEGY

Managing personal finances goes beyond simple budgeting and tracking expenses—it requires a well-thought-out strategy to maximize savings, investments, and long-term financial growth. Optimizing your financial strategy means making informed decisions about how you earn, spend, save, and invest, ensuring that your money is working efficiently for you. Whether you're looking to eliminate debt, build wealth, or prepare for retirement, refining your approach to money management can help you achieve financial stability and long-term success.

A strong financial strategy involves setting clear goals, leveraging advanced tools like Quicken, and making data-driven decisions. By analyzing spending patterns, adjusting budgets, tracking investments, and planning for future expenses, you can create a system that supports both your short-term needs and long-term aspirations. Additionally, incorporating smart tax planning, debt management, and automated financial processes can help reduce stress and improve overall financial health.

This section will guide you through advanced techniques for optimizing your financial approach, from fine-tuning your budget to leveraging investment insights. By implementing these strategies, you'll gain greater control over your finances and make more confident, informed decisions that align with your financial goals.

Using Forecasting Tools for Smarter Planning

Financial forecasting is a powerful strategy that helps you predict future income, expenses, and overall financial health. Instead of reacting to financial surprises, forecasting allows you to plan ahead, make informed decisions, and prepare for potential challenges. By using forecasting tools, you can estimate cash flow, anticipate upcoming expenses, and align your financial decisions with long-term goals.

Why Financial Forecasting Matters

1. **Better Budgeting** – Forecasting helps you see where your money is headed, allowing you to adjust your budget accordingly.

2. **Avoiding Cash Shortages** – Predicting expenses ensures you always have enough funds for essential bills and savings.

3. **Strategic Decision-Making** – Whether you're planning a big purchase, investment, or debt repayment, forecasting tools provide insights to make smart financial choices.

4. **Improved Savings and Investment Planning** – With an accurate forecast, you can set realistic savings goals and plan investments with confidence.

How Forecasting Tools Work in Quicken

Quicken offers several forecasting features that allow you to visualize your financial future based on your historical data and planned transactions. Some key tools include:

- **Cash Flow Forecasting** – Helps predict how much money you'll have in your accounts over time by analyzing scheduled bills, deposits, and recurring transactions.

- **Spending Trend Analysis** – Identifies spending patterns and suggests adjustments to keep you within budget.

- **Debt Payoff Planner** – Calculates how long it will take to pay off debts based on your repayment plan and interest rates.

- **Investment Projections** – Estimates future portfolio performance based on historical data and market trends.

Steps to Use Forecasting Tools Effectively

1. **Review Past Transactions** – Ensure that your financial records are up to date for accurate predictions.

2. **Set Future Income and Expenses** – Enter upcoming paychecks, bills, and expected expenditures to create a detailed forecast.

3. **Adjust Based on Goals** – If you're saving for a major expense or paying off debt, modify the forecast to see how different financial choices impact your future.

4. **Regularly Update Your Forecast** – Life changes, and so does your financial situation. Keep your forecast current to stay ahead of any shifts in income or expenses.

Maximizing the Benefits of Forecasting

- **Automate Bill Payments and Savings** – Use insights from your forecast to ensure bills are paid on time and savings goals are consistently met.

- **Plan for Emergencies** – Identify how much you need in an emergency fund by forecasting unexpected expenses.

- **Optimize Investments** – Use forecasting data to determine the best times to invest or rebalance your portfolio.

By leveraging forecasting tools, you can take control of your financial future with confidence, ensuring that every dollar is allocated wisely. Whether you're managing daily expenses or planning for long-term wealth, smarter forecasting will help you stay on track and achieve financial success.

Effective Debt Reduction Techniques

Managing debt efficiently is essential for achieving financial stability and long-term success. Without a clear strategy, debt can quickly become overwhelming, leading to unnecessary financial stress and high-interest payments. By implementing effective debt reduction techniques, you can regain control over your finances, reduce interest costs, and work toward becoming debt-free.

1. Assess Your Debt Situation

Before creating a repayment plan, it's crucial to take an honest look at your debts. List all outstanding balances, including credit cards, personal loans, mortgages, and any other obligations. Be sure to note:

- Total debt amount
- Interest rates
- Minimum monthly payments
- Loan terms

This will help you identify which debts are costing you the most and prioritize them accordingly.

2. Use the Debt Snowball or Debt Avalanche Method

Two of the most popular debt repayment strategies are:

- **Debt Snowball Method** – Focus on paying off the smallest debts first while making minimum payments on others. Once the smallest debt is cleared, apply that payment amount to the next smallest debt, creating momentum.

- **Debt Avalanche Method** – Prioritize debts with the highest interest rates first, while making minimum payments on others. This method saves the most money on interest in the long run.

Choose the method that best fits your financial goals and motivation style.

3. Consolidate Debt for Easier Management

Debt consolidation involves combining multiple debts into one loan with a lower interest rate. This can simplify repayments and reduce overall interest costs. Common consolidation options include:

- Balance transfer credit cards (with 0% introductory APR)

- Personal loans

- Home equity loans

Before consolidating, ensure that the new terms will truly save you money and not extend your repayment period unnecessarily.

4. Negotiate for Lower Interest Rates

Many lenders are willing to negotiate lower interest rates, especially if you have a good payment history. Contact creditors and ask about:

- Reduced interest rates

- Lower minimum payments

- Debt settlement options (if applicable)

Even a small reduction in interest can lead to significant savings over time.

5. Create a Realistic Repayment Plan

A structured repayment plan ensures you stay on track. Consider:

- Allocating extra funds (such as bonuses, tax refunds, or side income) toward debt payments

- Automating payments to avoid missed deadlines

- Setting debt-free milestones to stay motivated

6. Cut Unnecessary Expenses

Reducing discretionary spending can free up money for debt payments. Look for areas where you can cut back, such as:

- Dining out and entertainment

- Subscription services

- Impulse purchases

Redirecting these savings toward debt will accelerate your progress.

7. Increase Your Income

If possible, finding additional income sources can speed up debt repayment. Consider:

- Taking on freelance work or side gigs

- Selling unused items

- Asking for a raise or seeking a higher-paying job

Even a small increase in income can make a significant impact when applied directly to debt payments.

8. Avoid Accumulating New Debt

While working on debt reduction, it's essential to prevent further debt accumulation. To do this:

- Limit credit card usage and rely on cash or debit for purchases

- Build an emergency fund to avoid using credit for unexpected expenses

- Stick to a budget that prioritizes savings and essential expenses

9. Monitor Your Progress Regularly

Tracking your debt payoff progress can keep you motivated and help identify areas for improvement. Use financial tracking tools, such as Quicken, to:

- Monitor outstanding balances

- Track payments and interest charges

- Adjust your repayment strategy as needed

10. Stay Committed to a Debt-Free Future

Becoming debt-free is a journey that requires discipline and commitment. Once you've paid off your debts, continue practicing good financial habits by:

- Saving regularly

- Investing wisely

- Using credit responsibly

By following these effective debt reduction techniques, you can take control of your finances, reduce financial stress, and build a more secure future.

Setting and Achieving Retirement and Savings Goals

Planning for the future requires a proactive approach to saving and investing. Whether you're preparing for retirement, building an emergency fund, or working toward a specific financial goal, setting a clear strategy will help you stay on track. Effective savings habits and smart financial planning ensure that you achieve long-term security and financial independence.

1. Define Your Savings and Retirement Goals

Before setting up a savings plan, it's essential to identify what you're saving for. Common financial goals include:

- **Retirement** – Ensuring you have enough funds to maintain your lifestyle after you stop working.

- **Emergency Fund** – Covering unexpected expenses like medical bills, car repairs, or job loss.

- **Large Purchases** – Saving for a home, vehicle, or other major expense.

- **Education Funds** – Preparing for college tuition or further professional development.

Once you've defined your goals, assign a specific timeline and target amount to each one.

2. Determine How Much You Need to Save

For retirement planning, use the following factors to estimate your savings needs:

- **Desired retirement age** – The earlier you retire, the more savings you'll need.

- **Expected living expenses** – Factor in housing, healthcare, food, travel, and lifestyle choices.

- **Inflation rate** – Costs will rise over time, so adjust your savings accordingly.

- **Investment returns** – Consider the expected growth of your retirement accounts.

A common rule of thumb is to aim for at least 70-80% of your pre-retirement income per year during retirement. Use retirement calculators to estimate your required savings.

3. Choose the Right Savings and Investment Accounts

Selecting the right financial tools can maximize your savings potential. Consider these options:

- **Employer-Sponsored Retirement Plans** – 401(k) or 403(b) accounts with employer matching contributions.

- **Individual Retirement Accounts (IRAs)** – Traditional or Roth IRAs, offering tax advantages for long-term savings.

- **High-Yield Savings Accounts** – Ideal for emergency funds and short-term savings.

- **Investment Accounts** – Stocks, bonds, mutual funds, and real estate to grow your wealth over time.

Diversifying your investments ensures a balanced approach to achieving financial security.

4. Automate Your Savings

To stay consistent, set up automatic contributions to your savings and retirement accounts. This ensures that you prioritize savings before spending. Strategies include:

- **Payroll deductions** – Directly contributing to a retirement plan from your paycheck.

- **Scheduled transfers** – Setting up recurring transfers from checking to savings or investment accounts.

- **Round-up savings apps** – Automatically saving spare change from everyday purchases.

5. Monitor and Adjust Your Plan Regularly

Your financial situation may change over time, requiring adjustments to your savings strategy. Review your progress at least annually by:

- Checking retirement account balances and growth rates.

- Reassessing financial goals based on life changes (marriage, children, career shifts).

- Increasing contributions as your income grows.

6. Reduce Debt to Maximize Savings

High-interest debt can slow down your savings progress. Prioritize debt reduction to free up more income for long-term financial goals. Consider strategies such as:

- Paying off credit card debt before increasing retirement contributions.

- Refinancing loans for lower interest rates.

- Using windfalls (bonuses, tax refunds) to reduce outstanding balances.

7. Plan for Taxes and Withdrawal Strategies

Understanding tax implications is essential when withdrawing retirement funds. Strategies to minimize tax burdens include:

- Withdrawing from taxable accounts before tax-advantaged accounts.

- Using required minimum distributions (RMDs) efficiently.

- Converting traditional IRAs to Roth IRAs for tax-free withdrawals in retirement.

Consulting a financial advisor can help you optimize tax-efficient withdrawal plans.

8. Stay Committed to Long-Term Financial Success

Building a strong retirement and savings plan requires patience and consistency. Stay focused on your goals by:

- Avoiding impulsive financial decisions.

- Continuing to invest during market fluctuations.

- Revisiting your plan regularly to ensure alignment with your evolving financial situation.

By setting clear savings goals, making smart investment choices, and maintaining discipline, you can secure a comfortable retirement and achieve lasting financial freedom.

Quicken for Small Business Owners

Managing business finances effectively is critical for small business owners. With multiple income sources, expenses, invoices, and tax obligations, keeping track of financial data can become overwhelming without the right tools. Quicken provides small business owners with a streamlined solution for tracking income and expenses, managing cash flow, and generating reports—all in one platform.

1. Organizing Business Finances Efficiently

Quicken allows small business owners to separate personal and business finances, ensuring clear financial records. Key organizational features include:

- **Categorization of transactions** – Assign income and expenses to specific business categories.

- **Multiple account management** – Track business checking, savings, and credit card accounts in one place.

- **Cloud synchronization** – Access financial data across devices for on-the-go business management.

By maintaining well-organized records, business owners can make informed financial decisions and ensure compliance with tax regulations.

2. Tracking Income and Expenses

Accurate income and expense tracking is essential for profitability and tax reporting. Quicken simplifies this process by:

- **Automatically importing transactions** from bank accounts, credit cards, and payment processors.

- **Tagging transactions** based on projects, clients, or business activities.

- **Generating profit and loss statements** to assess business performance.

By keeping a real-time record of financial activity, business owners can monitor cash flow and adjust their budget accordingly.

3. Managing Invoices and Payments

Quicken offers invoice management tools that help businesses stay on top of payments. Features include:

- **Invoice creation and tracking** – Customize invoices, send them to clients, and track outstanding payments.

- **Payment reminders** – Get notifications for due and overdue invoices.

- **Integration with online payment options** – Accept digital payments for faster transactions.

Timely invoicing and payment tracking help improve cash flow and maintain healthy financial operations.

4. Budgeting and Cash Flow Management

A well-structured budget ensures financial stability and business growth. With Quicken, business owners can:

- **Set up business budgets** based on projected income and expenses.

- **Monitor cash flow trends** to anticipate shortfalls and surpluses.

- **Adjust spending and investment plans** to optimize financial resources.

This proactive approach helps businesses maintain profitability and prevent financial difficulties.

5. Tax Preparation and Deductions

Quicken simplifies tax preparation by organizing financial records and identifying potential deductions. Business owners can:

- **Categorize tax-deductible expenses** such as office supplies, travel, and utilities.

- **Generate tax reports** including Schedule C and profit/loss summaries.

- **Export financial data** for seamless integration with tax software or accountants.

By keeping accurate records throughout the year, businesses can maximize deductions and ensure smooth tax filing.

6. Generating Business Reports for Decision-Making

Quicken provides insightful reports that help business owners analyze financial performance. Some useful reports include:

- **Profit and Loss Reports** – Assess revenue, expenses, and net income.

- **Balance Sheet Reports** – View assets, liabilities, and equity.

- **Expense Reports** – Track spending patterns and identify cost-saving opportunities.

These reports offer valuable insights that support informed business decisions and strategic planning.

7. Payroll and Employee Expense Management

For businesses with employees, Quicken helps track payroll expenses and reimbursements. Business owners can:

- **Record payroll transactions** to ensure accurate bookkeeping.

- **Monitor employee expense reimbursements** for tax and budget purposes.

- **Generate payroll-related reports** for compliance and financial review.

Keeping payroll and employee expenses organized ensures regulatory compliance and smooth financial operations.

8. Planning for Business Growth

Quickens financial tracking tools allow small business owners to set growth targets and assess progress. With data-driven insights, businesses can:

- **Identify profitable areas** and invest accordingly.

- **Manage debt and funding options** for expansion.

- **Develop long-term financial strategies** based on historical trends.

By leveraging Quickens features, small business owners can optimize their financial management, reduce manual bookkeeping efforts, and focus on scaling their business.

Quicken is a powerful financial tool that simplifies business accounting, enhances cash flow visibility, and supports better financial decision-making. Whether tracking daily transactions, managing invoices, or preparing taxes, small business owners can benefit from the efficiency and accuracy that Quicken offers. By integrating this software into their workflow, entrepreneurs can stay financially organized and drive long-term business success.

CHAPTER 6

TRANSITIONING TO QUICKEN

Making the switch to Quicken can be a game-changer for individuals and business owners looking to streamline their financial management. Whether you are moving from manual tracking methods, spreadsheets, or another financial software, Quicken provides a comprehensive and user-friendly solution that simplifies budgeting, expense tracking, bill management, and investment monitoring—all in one place. Transitioning to a new financial management system may seem overwhelming at first, but with the right approach, the process can be smooth and hassle-free. This section will guide you through key steps such as setting up your accounts, importing financial data, customizing categories, and optimizing Quickens features to fit your financial needs. By following a structured approach, you can quickly adapt to Quicken and take full advantage of its powerful tools to gain better control over your finances.

Adapting to a Digital Financial System

As technology continues to evolve, traditional financial management methods—such as paper records, manual spreadsheets, and checkbook balancing—are being replaced by digital solutions. A digital financial system offers greater efficiency, accuracy, and convenience, enabling users to manage their finances in real-time with automated tracking, reporting, and forecasting tools. However, adapting to this transition requires a shift in mindset and a willingness to embrace new processes.

1. Understanding the Benefits of a Digital Financial System

Switching to a digital system like Quicken provides several advantages:

- **Automation** – Transactions can be imported directly from bank accounts, reducing manual entry.

- **Organization** – Categorizing income and expenses simplifies tracking and budgeting.

- **Accessibility** – Cloud-based options allow users to manage finances from anywhere.

- **Security** – Digital financial tools offer encryption and backup features to protect sensitive data.

- **Insightful Reporting** – Real-time financial reports help users make informed decisions.

By leveraging these benefits, users can save time and improve financial efficiency.

2. Setting Up a Digital System for Success

Adapting to a digital financial system involves more than just installing software—it requires structuring financial data for seamless management. Key steps include:

- **Consolidating financial accounts** into one platform for streamlined tracking.

- **Importing historical financial data** to maintain a complete financial picture.

- **Customizing categories and tags** for accurate reporting and analysis.

- **Setting up alerts and reminders** to avoid missed payments and overdrafts.

A well-organized setup ensures a smooth transition and makes the system more effective.

3. Overcoming Common Challenges

Some users may face initial difficulties when transitioning to a digital system, such as:

- **Learning new software features** – Taking time to explore Quicken's tools can ease the learning curve.

- **Adjusting to automated tracking** – While automation reduces errors, it requires regular monitoring.

- **Managing security concerns** – Using strong passwords and two-factor authentication enhances data security.

By addressing these challenges proactively, users can adapt more easily and take full advantage of digital financial management.

4. Developing a Routine for Digital Financial Management

Consistency is key when using a digital financial system. To maintain financial accuracy and control, users should:

- **Review transactions regularly** to ensure accuracy and proper categorization.

- **Monitor cash flow and budgets** to stay on top of spending.

- **Generate reports periodically** to assess financial progress and adjust plans.

- **Back up data frequently** to prevent loss of critical financial information.

By incorporating these habits, users can optimize their financial management and make more informed financial decisions.

Adapting to a digital financial system is a crucial step toward modernizing financial management. While the transition may take some time, the long-term benefits—such as efficiency, accuracy, and better financial insights—make it a worthwhile investment. By leveraging tools like Quicken, users can simplify their financial processes, gain better control over their money, and work toward achieving their financial goals with confidence.

Making the Most of Quickens Capabilities

Quicken is more than just a financial tracking tool—it's a comprehensive system designed to help users take full control of their finances with powerful features for budgeting, investment tracking, bill management, and long-term financial planning. To maximize its potential, users should explore its advanced capabilities and tailor them to their unique financial needs.

1. Automating Financial Tasks for Efficiency

One of Quickens most valuable features is automation, which reduces manual work and ensures accuracy. Users can:

- **Link bank accounts and credit cards** for automatic transaction imports.

- **Set up bill reminders and autopay** to avoid late fees.

- **Schedule recurring transactions** to track regular income and expenses effortlessly.

By automating financial management, users can save time while maintaining accuracy in their records.

2. Customizing Categories and Tags for Better Tracking

To gain meaningful insights into spending habits, users should personalize their financial categories and tags. Quicken allows:

- **Custom categories** to reflect specific expense types (e.g., "Freelance Income" instead of just "Income").

- **Tags for deeper analysis**, such as categorizing expenses by project, household member, or business purpose.

- **Splitting transactions** to allocate expenses across multiple categories.

This level of detail makes it easier to track where money is going and make informed financial decisions.

3. Leveraging Budgeting Tools for Smarter Money Management

Quickens budgeting tools allow users to create realistic financial plans and track spending in real time. Users can:

- **Set monthly or yearly budgets** based on past spending habits.

- **Use the rollover feature** to carry over unused budgeted amounts.

- **Receive alerts** when approaching or exceeding budget limits.

With these tools, users can stay on track with their financial goals and avoid overspending.

4. Maximizing Investment Tracking and Analysis

For those managing investments, Quicken provides powerful tracking and reporting tools, including:

- **Real-time portfolio updates** by linking brokerage accounts.

- **Detailed performance analysis** to compare investments against market benchmarks.

- **Capital gains tracking** for tax planning and reporting.

By using Quickens investment features, users can make better decisions to grow their wealth.

5. Generating Custom Financial Reports

Quicken offers a variety of financial reports that provide a clear picture of income, expenses, net worth, and more. Users can:

- **Customize reports** to focus on specific accounts, categories, or time periods.

- **Compare financial trends** over time to adjust spending habits.

- **Export data** for tax preparation or financial planning discussions.

These reports help users make data-driven decisions and improve financial management.

6. Using Quicken Mobile and Cloud Features for Accessibility

Quicken isn't just for desktop use—it offers mobile and cloud-based features that enhance convenience. Users can:

- **Sync data across devices** to access finances from anywhere.

- **Use the mobile app** to track expenses on the go.

- **Enable secure cloud backups** to prevent data loss.

By taking advantage of these features, users can manage their finances anytime, anywhere.

7. Staying Secure with Data Protection Features

Financial data security is critical, and Quicken provides built-in protection tools, such as:

- **Password-protected files** to keep sensitive information secure.

- **Two-factor authentication** for added security when accessing accounts.

- **Encrypted cloud storage** to protect backups from unauthorized access.

By implementing these security measures, users can confidently manage their finances without risk.

Quicken is a robust financial management tool, but its true power lies in how users leverage its features. By automating transactions, customizing categories, tracking investments, generating insightful reports, and using mobile access, users can maximize Quickens capabilities to gain full control over their financial future. Taking the time to explore and apply these features ensures a more efficient, organized, and stress-free approach to personal and business finance management.

CHAPTER 7

AVOIDING COMMON MISTAKES

Managing finances effectively with Quicken requires more than just using the software—it's about using it correctly. While Quicken simplifies financial tracking, budgeting, and planning, many users make common mistakes that can lead to inaccurate records, missed payments, or poor financial decisions. Whether it's neglecting regular updates, mis categorizing transactions, or failing to back up data, these errors can undermine the effectiveness of the system.

This section will highlight the most frequent mistakes Quicken users make and provide actionable strategies to avoid them. By understanding these pitfalls and learning best practices, you can ensure accurate financial tracking, maintain better control over your money, and make smarter financial decisions.

The Most Frequent Quicken Errors and How to Fix Them

While Quicken is a powerful financial tool, users can occasionally encounter errors that may disrupt their financial tracking. These errors, however, are often easy to fix with a bit of knowledge and a systematic approach. Identifying and resolving these issues quickly ensures that your financial records remain accurate and up-to-date.

1. Incorrect Transaction Categorization

One of the most common errors in Quicken is categorizing transactions incorrectly. Whether it's misclassifying income or expenses, or placing a personal expense in a business category, this can lead to inaccurate reports and budgeting issues.

How to Fix It:

- **Recheck Categories**: Review your transactions regularly to ensure they're categorized correctly.

- **Use Custom Categories**: Create specific categories that fit your needs, making it easier to assign the correct label.

- **Split Transactions**: If a single transaction covers multiple categories, use the split feature to allocate the amounts accurately.

2. Duplicate Transactions

Occasionally, Quicken may import duplicate transactions from linked accounts, especially when syncing with banks or credit cards. This can lead to an inflated account balance and skewed reports.

How to Fix It:

- **Identify and Delete Duplicates**: Go through your transactions and remove any duplicates manually or by using Quickens "Find and Fix Errors" feature.

- **Check Account Settings**: Make sure your bank feeds are set up correctly to prevent multiple imports of the same transaction.

- **Reconcile Accounts Regularly**: Regular reconciliation helps identify duplicates and other discrepancies early.

3. Incorrect Account Balances

Another common issue is incorrect account balances, which can occur when transactions aren't entered or synced correctly. This can lead to errors in budgeting and financial planning.

How to Fix It:

- **Reconcile Accounts**: Regularly reconcile each account with your bank statement to ensure balances match.

- **Manually Adjust Transactions**: If you find a missing or incorrect transaction, add or adjust it manually.

- **Check for Unmatched Transactions**: If a transaction hasn't been matched with a downloaded one, make sure it's properly linked.

4. Overlooking Regular Updates and Syncs

Not syncing your Quicken accounts regularly with your bank can lead to outdated or incomplete financial data. Transactions from recent purchases, deposits, or payments might not appear, making it hard to manage your finances.

How to Fix It:

- **Set Up Automatic Sync**: Ensure your accounts are set to sync automatically, so your financial data is always up to date.

- **Manually Sync Accounts**: If you notice discrepancies, manually sync your accounts to refresh your data.

- **Review Bank Feed Settings**: Ensure that your bank feeds are working correctly to avoid missing or delayed transactions.

5. Budgeting Errors

Improper budget setup, such as incorrectly allocated budget limits or overlooked categories, is a frequent issue. This can result in inaccurate spending reports and missed financial targets.

How to Fix It:

- **Review and Adjust Budgets Regularly**: Set up your budget based on realistic income and expense estimates. Revisit it periodically to make adjustments as needed.

- **Utilize Budget Alerts**: Use Quicken's alert feature to notify you when you are nearing or exceeding budget limits.

- **Break Down Complex Expenses**: For large or irregular expenses, break them down into smaller, manageable categories to ensure accuracy.

6. Not Backing Up Data

Failing to back up your Quicken data can result in the loss of important financial information due to software crashes, hardware failures, or other technical issues.

How to Fix It:

- **Back Up Regularly**: Make it a habit to back up your Quicken data at least once a week.

- **Use Cloud Backups**: Enable cloud backup options to ensure your data is protected and easily accessible.

- **Set Up Auto Backups**: Configure Quicken to back up automatically, minimizing the risk of data loss.

7. Ignoring Tax Implications

Quicken can help track tax-related expenses, but users sometimes overlook tax reporting features, leading to confusion when preparing for tax season.

How to Fix It:

- **Categorize Tax-Related Expenses**: Set up specific categories for deductible expenses and track them consistently throughout the year.

- **Use Tax Reports**: Take advantage of Quickens tax reports to get an overview of potential deductions and tax liabilities.

- **Stay Informed on Tax Changes**: Review your tax settings periodically and adjust categories as tax laws or personal circumstances change.

8. Mismanagement of Investments

Investment tracking can sometimes lead to errors in calculating returns, dividends, or capital gains, which can distort financial planning and reporting.

How to Fix It:

- **Update Investment Data**: Make sure your investments are updated with the latest transactions, including buys, sells, and dividends.

- **Track Portfolio Performance**: Regularly review and adjust your portfolio to ensure accurate performance tracking.

- **Reconcile Investment Accounts**: Reconcile investment accounts at least quarterly to ensure that data from brokerage firms matches your Quicken records.

Quicken is a powerful tool for managing your finances, but like any software, errors can occur. By staying proactive in identifying and correcting these common mistakes, you can ensure that your financial data remains accurate and up-to-date. Regularly reviewing your transactions, syncing accounts, and leveraging Quickens built-in tools for error detection can go a long way in optimizing your financial management. With a few simple steps, you can avoid these pitfalls and make the most of Quickens capabilities to maintain a strong and organized financial life.

Best Practices for Efficient and Error-Free Management

To fully harness the power of Quicken and ensure your financial management is both efficient and error-free, it's essential to implement best practices. By following proven methods for data entry, organization, and regular maintenance, you can streamline your financial workflow and avoid common pitfalls. These best practices will not only save you time but also help you maintain accurate records and make better financial decisions.

1. Regularly Reconcile Accounts

Reconciliation is a key practice in maintaining the accuracy of your financial records. Regularly reconciling your accounts ensures that the transactions in Quicken match those in your bank or credit card statements, helping to identify errors and discrepancies early on.

Best Practice:

- Reconcile each account at least once a month. This ensures that all transactions are accounted for and balances are correct.

- If you notice discrepancies, investigate them immediately and correct any errors to maintain accurate records.

2. Automate Transaction Imports

One of the most time-consuming aspects of financial management is entering transactions manually. Quicken offers the ability to automatically import transactions from linked bank accounts and credit cards, saving you time and reducing the risk of human error.

Best Practice:

- Link all your financial accounts to Quicken, so transactions are automatically imported.

- Regularly check for missing or duplicate transactions to ensure the data is correct.

3. Categorize Transactions Consistently

Accurate categorization of transactions is essential for generating meaningful financial reports and maintaining an organized budget. Consistently assigning transactions to the correct categories ensures that your spending analysis is precise and helps you track your financial goals effectively.

Best Practice:

- Set up clear and customized categories that align with your financial needs.

- Review your categories periodically and adjust as needed.

- Use Quickens "Split" feature for transactions that fall under multiple categories (e.g., a combined personal and business purchase).

4. Set Up and Stick to a Budget

A solid budget is the foundation of efficient financial management. Quicken offers powerful budgeting tools that allow you to set spending limits and track your progress in real-time. Setting up a budget and sticking to it is crucial to avoiding overspending and staying on top of your financial goals.

Best Practice:

- Create a budget based on your actual income and regular expenses.

- Set realistic limits for each category to ensure you don't overextend yourself.

- Regularly review your budget to make adjustments as your financial situation evolves.

5. Regularly Back Up Your Data

Losing your financial data can be catastrophic, especially if you don't have a recent backup. Quicken provides options to back up your data automatically or manually, ensuring that your records are safe.

Best Practice:

- Back up your Quicken data regularly to an external drive or cloud storage.

- Enable automatic backups within Quicken to ensure your data is always protected.

- Store backups in multiple locations to safeguard against potential data loss.

6. Utilize Quickens Reporting Tools

Quickens reporting tools allow you to generate detailed financial reports, which can be used for analysis, planning, and tax preparation. These reports provide a comprehensive view of your financial situation and can help you make informed decisions.

Best Practice:

- Generate monthly or quarterly financial reports to track income, expenses, and overall financial health.

- Use tax-specific reports to keep track of deductible expenses throughout the year.

- Customize reports to focus on specific categories or accounts to gain deeper insights into your financial habits.

7. Keep Your Software Updated

Quicken regularly releases updates to improve performance, fix bugs, and introduce new features. Ensuring that your Quicken software is up to date is crucial for efficient operation and error-free management.

Best Practice:

- Set up automatic updates to ensure that your software is always running the latest version.

- Periodically check for manual updates if automatic updates are disabled.

- Review release notes for any new features that could improve your financial management.

8. Use Security Features to Protect Your Data

Financial data is sensitive and needs to be protected against unauthorized access. Quicken offers security features, including password protection and two-factor authentication, to safeguard your information.

Best Practice:

- Use a strong password to protect your Quicken file and enable two-factor authentication for an added layer of security.

- Lock your financial file with a password to prevent unauthorized access.

- Regularly monitor your accounts for unusual activity and report any suspicious behavior to your bank or credit card provider.

9. Review and Adjust Regularly

Your financial situation is constantly changing, whether due to shifts in income, lifestyle, or financial goals. Regularly reviewing and adjusting your financial records, budgets, and goals ensures that Quicken continues to align with your current needs.

Best Practice:

- Review your accounts and transactions on a monthly basis to ensure everything is accurate.

- Adjust your budget as needed based on any changes in income or expenses.

- Set new financial goals annually and track your progress toward achieving them.

10. Leverage Quickens Mobile App

Quickens mobile app allows you to manage your finances on the go. Whether you're at the store, on vacation, or working remotely, having access to your financial data can help you stay on top of your finances in real-time.

Best Practice:

- Download the Quicken mobile app and sync it with your desktop version to manage your finances from anywhere.

- Use the mobile app to capture receipts, check account balances, and track spending while you're away from your computer.

By adopting these best practices, you can maximize Quickens capabilities and ensure efficient, error-free financial management. Regular reconciliation, consistent categorization, data backups, and leveraging reporting tools will help keep your financial records accurate and provide deeper insights into your financial health. With these strategies in place, you'll be able to use Quicken with confidence and stay on track toward achieving your financial goals.

CHAPTER 8

USER SUCCESS STORIES

One of the most powerful ways to understand the true potential of Quicken is through the experiences of those who have used it to transform their financial lives. User success stories highlight the practical applications and benefits that come with mastering the software. These stories provide real-world examples of individuals and businesses who have navigated financial challenges, streamlined their finances, and achieved their financial goals with the help of Quicken. Whether it's eliminating debt, building wealth, or gaining better control over spending, these success stories offer inspiration and insights for users at all levels. In this section, we'll explore how different users have successfully integrated Quicken into their financial strategies and the positive impacts it has had on their financial journey.

Real-Life Case Studies of Quicken Users

Real-Life Case Studies of Quicken Users

Quicken has helped countless users streamline their finances, eliminate debt, and plan for a secure financial future. From individuals tracking everyday expenses to small business owners managing complex accounting needs, Quickens versatile tools have proven valuable across various financial situations. Below are some real-life case studies that highlight the practical ways Quicken has empowered users to take control of their finances and achieve their goals.

Case Study 1: Sarah, A Busy Professional Who Paid Off Her Debt

Background:

Sarah, a 32-year-old marketing manager, was struggling to keep up with her growing debt, which included student loans, credit card balances, and a car loan. She felt overwhelmed by the number of payments she had to make each month and was unsure of where to begin in reducing her debt.

How Quicken Helped:

Sarah turned to Quicken for help in organizing her finances and creating a plan to pay off her debt. She used Quickens budgeting features to categorize her expenses and track her income, which gave her a clear picture of her financial situation. With Quickens Debt Reduction Planner, Sarah was able to prioritize high-interest debts and create a personalized repayment strategy.

Outcome:

Within 18 months, Sarah was able to pay off her credit card debt and student loans, and she set up a savings plan for emergencies. Quickens reminders and alerts helped her stay on track with her payments, and her overall financial confidence increased as she saw her debts shrink and savings grow.

Case Study 2: Mark and Lisa, Newlyweds Building Their First Home

Background:

Mark and Lisa, a young couple in their late twenties, had recently gotten married and were eager to build their first home. While they both had stable jobs, they found it difficult to save for a down payment while managing their daily expenses, student loans, and car payments.

How Quicken Helped:

Using Quickens "Goal Setting" feature, Mark and Lisa were able to set up a savings goal for their down payment and track their progress over time. By linking their bank accounts to Quicken, they automatically tracked every expense, allowing them to identify areas where they could cut back. Additionally, quickens reports helped them evaluate their spending habits and adjust their budget accordingly.

Outcome:

Within a year, Mark and Lisa were able to save enough for a 20% down payment on a home. They used Quickens investment tracking tools to monitor their growing savings and even started contributing to a retirement account. Their success in budgeting and planning helped them feel confident about their financial future and set the foundation for building wealth.

Case Study 3: James, A Freelance Graphic Designer Managing Irregular Income

Background:

James is a freelance graphic designer whose income fluctuates monthly, making it difficult to manage his finances. Some months, he earned well, while others were slower, leaving him anxious about his ability to cover his living expenses.

How Quicken Helped:

James used Quickens "Irregular Income" feature to manage his variable earnings. By setting up separate categories for different types of income, he was able to estimate his monthly income range and adjust his budget to reflect the most recent earnings. Additionally, he used Quickens "Bill Pay" function to schedule payments in advance, ensuring he never missed a due date.

Outcome:

James found that Quicken helped him create a flexible but structured budget that allowed him to manage his irregular income with ease. By planning for leaner months and automating bill payments, he was able to save for future business expenses, avoid financial stress, and focus more on growing his design business.

Case Study 4: Jessica, A Small Business Owner Keeping Track of Cash Flow

Background:

Jessica owns a small boutique that sells handmade jewelry. As her business grew, managing her business finances became increasingly difficult. She struggled to separate personal and business expenses, which made tracking her cash flow and preparing taxes challenging.

How Quicken Helped:

Jessica decided to use Quicken for her small business. She linked her business bank account and credit cards to the software, enabling automatic transaction downloads. Quickens "Business Income and Expense Tracker" allowed her to keep track of all sales and expenses, and the software automatically categorized transactions into the correct business categories, helping her maintain clear financial records.

Outcome:

Quicken allowed Jessica to easily track her business cash flow, monitor profit margins, and identify areas for improvement. She also used the software's tax-related features to prepare her quarterly tax filings, saving her time and reducing errors. With Quickens help, Jessica was able to scale her business while maintaining a clear financial picture.

Case Study 5: Tom, A Retiree Planning for the Future

Background:

Tom, a 65-year-old retiree, wanted to ensure that his retirement savings would last throughout his golden years. After years of working, he now had a fixed income and wanted to optimize his spending while maintaining a comfortable lifestyle.

How Quicken Helped:

Tom used Quickens "Retirement Planning" tools to project his future spending and calculate how long his savings would last at different rates of withdrawal. He also used Quickens budgeting tools to track his monthly expenses, ensuring that he stayed within his means. The software's "Investment Tracking" feature helped Tom monitor his retirement account performance and adjust his withdrawals as needed.

Outcome:

Tom felt confident that his retirement savings would last well into his 80s. By regularly reviewing his spending and adjusting his financial strategy based on Quickens reports, Tom was able to enjoy his retirement without the stress of financial uncertainty.

These case studies show the diverse ways in which Quicken can be used to achieve financial success. Whether you're paying off debt, saving for a home, managing business finances, or planning for retirement, Quicken offers the tools to help you navigate life's financial challenges. Real-life users have experienced tangible benefits from the software, enabling them to achieve their financial goals and secure their futures. Your financial journey is unique, but with the right tools and strategies, success is within reach.

CHAPTER 9

TROUBLESHOOTING AND BEST PRACTICES

No financial software is perfect, and even the most experienced users may occasionally encounter challenges. Whether you're dealing with syncing issues, incorrect transaction data, or other technical glitches, understanding how to troubleshoot effectively can save you time and frustration. In this section, we'll dive into some common troubleshooting tips for Quicken users and highlight best practices to ensure you're getting the most out of your software. By following these strategies, you can keep your financial records running smoothly, avoid errors, and make the most of Quickens powerful features. Whether you're a beginner or an advanced user, these tips will help you resolve issues quickly and maintain a hassle-free financial experience.

Resolving Common Issues and Errors

While Quicken is designed to simplify your financial management, it's not uncommon to encounter occasional issues or errors. Whether it's syncing problems, incorrect balances, or transaction discrepancies, knowing how to troubleshoot these issues effectively can save you a lot of time and hassle. Here's a guide to resolving some of the most common problems Quicken users face:

1. Bank Account Syncing Issues

Problem: Quicken isn't syncing with your bank account or financial institution.

Solution:

- **Check your internet connection** to ensure it's stable.

- **Update Quicken** to the latest version. Quicken regularly releases updates to improve compatibility with financial institutions.

- **Disconnect and reconnect your account**. Sometimes, a simple disconnection and reconnection can resolve syncing issues.

- **Check the bank's website** to confirm if there's any temporary outage or system maintenance.

- If the issue persists, try **resetting the account connection** by going to Tools > Account List, selecting the account, and clicking the Edit button, then choosing "Update Now."

2. Duplicate Transactions

Problem: You notice duplicate transactions in your register.

Solution:

- **Review the import settings**. Quicken automatically downloads transactions from your bank, but if you have set up automatic transaction downloads and also manually entered the same transaction, duplicates can occur.

- **Use the "Find and Delete Duplicates" feature**. Go to Tools > Check for Duplicates to identify and remove duplicate entries.

- **Reconcile your accounts**. Regularly reconciling your accounts ensures that your records match your banks, helping you catch errors early.

3. Incorrect Account Balances

Problem: Your Quicken account balance doesn't match your actual bank account balance.

Solution:

- **Reconcile your account**. Go to Tools > Reconcile, and compare your Quicken register to your bank statement. This will help you identify discrepancies.

- **Look for unrecorded transactions**. If a transaction is missing in Quicken or entered incorrectly, it can affect your balance. Ensure all transactions are entered and categorized correctly.

- **Check for deleted or altered transactions**. Sometimes transactions might accidentally be deleted or modified. Use the "Undo" feature or check your transaction history to restore or fix any changes.

4. Missing or Incorrect Categories

Problem: Transactions are not categorized correctly, or categories are missing.

Solution:

- **Review category settings**. Go to Tools > Category List to ensure all categories are set up correctly. You can edit existing categories or create new ones as needed.

- **Use the "Assign Category" option**. If Quicken didn't automatically categorize a transaction correctly, you can manually assign the correct category by editing the transaction.

- **Customize your categories**. If the default categories don't suit your needs, Quicken allows you to create and customize your own categories for better financial organization.

5. Quicken Crashing or Freezing

Problem: Quicken freezes or crashes unexpectedly.

Solution:

- **Ensure Quicken is updated**. Make sure you're using the latest version of Quicken to avoid bugs and issues that may have been fixed in newer releases.

- **Check system requirements**. Ensure your computer meets the minimum system requirements for running Quicken smoothly. If your hardware is outdated, consider upgrading.

- **Run Quicken as an administrator**. Right-click the Quicken icon and select "Run as administrator" to avoid permission-related issues that may cause the software to crash.

- **Clear temporary files**. Temporary files can sometimes cause Quicken to perform slowly or crash. Clear these files via Tools > Validate and Repair > Repair Data File.

6. Error Messages During Online Banking or Bill Pay

Problem: Error messages when attempting to use online banking or bill pay features.

Solution:

- **Verify account settings**. Ensure your login credentials for your bank or bill pay services are entered correctly. You may need to re-enter or update these settings.

- **Check for service outages**. Verify with your bank or financial institution if they are experiencing outages that may prevent online banking services from functioning.

- **Update your bank connection**. Go to Tools > Account List, select the account, and click on the Edit button, then choose "Update Now" to refresh the bank connection and resolve errors.

7. Quicken Not Updating Transactions Automatically

Problem: Quicken is not downloading transactions automatically as expected.

Solution:

- **Check your online banking settings**. Ensure you have set up automatic downloads correctly by going to Account > Online Services and checking the connection settings.

- **Manually download transactions**. If automatic downloads are not working, you can manually download transactions from your bank's website and import them into Quicken.

- **Enable automatic transaction updates**. Go to Tools > Preferences > Online Banking, and make sure that automatic transaction downloads are enabled.

8. Data File Errors

Problem: Quicken reports an error when opening or working with a data file.

Solution:

- **Use the Repair Data feature**. Go to File > File Operations > Validate and Repair to fix errors in the data file.

- **Backup and restore your data**. If the repair feature doesn't work, try restoring a backup file from an earlier date when the data file was functioning correctly.

- **Create a new file**. If the data file is severely corrupted, you may need to create a new file and import your transactions into it.

By following these solutions, most common issues in Quicken can be easily resolved. Regular maintenance, such as updating your software, reconciling accounts, and backing up your data, can also prevent issues from arising in the future. Troubleshooting doesn't have to be a daunting task, and with these steps, you can keep your Quicken experience smooth and efficient.

Protecting Your Financial Data

Your financial data is one of your most valuable assets, and safeguarding it should be a top priority when using Quicken or any other financial management tool. Ensuring that your sensitive information—such as account balances, transaction history, and personal details—remains secure is crucial not only to prevent unauthorized access but also to avoid identity theft or fraud. Here's a guide to help you protect your financial data while using Quicken:

1. Use Strong Passwords

Why: Weak passwords are one of the most common ways for unauthorized users to gain access to your accounts.

How:

- **Create unique, strong passwords** for your Quicken account, financial institutions, and any linked accounts.

- Ensure your password is a mix of uppercase and lowercase letters, numbers, and special characters. Avoid easily guessed phrases like your name or birthdate.

- **Enable multi-factor authentication (MFA)** wherever possible. This adds an extra layer of protection by requiring you to confirm your identity through an additional method, such as a one-time code sent to your phone.

2. Regular Backups

Why: Data loss can occur due to hardware failures, software crashes, or other unforeseen events. Having a backup ensures that you won't lose important financial records.

How:

- **Backup your Quicken data regularly.** Quicken provides an option to back up your data automatically or manually, so take advantage of this feature.

- **Store backups in multiple locations** (e.g., external drives, cloud storage) for added security.

- Make sure your backups are encrypted to prevent unauthorized access.

3. Use Encryption

Why: Encrypting your financial data ensures that it's unreadable to anyone who doesn't have the proper decryption key.

How:

- **Enable encryption in Quicken** by selecting the option to encrypt your data file. This will ensure that your financial information is secured.

- If you're storing backups, use encryption software to protect these files before saving them to cloud storage or external drives.

4. Keep Software Up-to-Date

Why: Software updates often include security patches that fix vulnerabilities and prevent potential exploits.

How:

- **Regularly update Quicken** to ensure you have the latest features and security enhancements.

- Enable automatic updates so you never miss important security patches.

5. Be Cautious with Online Transactions

Why: Online banking and bill payments can expose you to phishing attacks or data theft if not handled securely.

How:

- Only **access your financial accounts on trusted, secure devices**. Avoid using public computers or untrusted networks when managing your financial data.

- **Double-check website URLs** to ensure you're on a legitimate site before entering any sensitive information.

- **Watch out for phishing attempts.** Don't click on links or open attachments in unsolicited emails or messages that appear to be from your bank or financial institutions. Instead, contact your bank directly if you suspect any fraudulent activity.

6. Limit Access to Your Financial Data

Why: Limiting who can access your financial information minimizes the risk of it being exposed or misused.

How:

- **Set up user access restrictions** in Quicken to control who can view or edit certain financial records.

- **Password-protect your Quicken file** to prevent unauthorized users from accessing your financial data.

- **Don't share your Quicken login credentials** with others unless absolutely necessary, and be cautious when providing your bank details.

7. Monitor Financial Accounts Regularly

Why: Regular monitoring of your bank accounts helps you spot unauthorized transactions early, minimizing potential damage.

How:

- **Reconcile your accounts** frequently to ensure all transactions are accurate and legitimate. This also helps you spot discrepancies that could indicate fraudulent activity.

- Set up **account alerts** with your bank to receive notifications of any large or unusual transactions, adding an extra layer of security.

8. Use Antivirus and Anti-malware Software

Why: Malware and viruses can infect your device and steal sensitive information, including your financial data.

How:

- Install and **keep antivirus and anti-malware software up to date** on any device you use to access Quicken.

- Run **regular scans** to identify and remove any potential threats.

9. Avoid Storing Sensitive Information in Quicken

Why: Although Quicken allows you to store some personal information (like credit card numbers and passwords), this can put your data at risk if your system is compromised.

How:

- **Limit the sensitive information stored in Quicken.** Instead, use a **secure password manager** to store sensitive details, such as login credentials, and only input the minimum necessary data in Quicken.

10. Protect Your Devices

Why: If your devices are compromised, your financial data becomes vulnerable.

How:

- **Lock your devices** with a password, PIN, or biometric security (fingerprint or facial recognition) to prevent unauthorized access.

- **Install a device tracker** or remote-wipe software in case your device is lost or stolen.

By implementing these strategies, you can ensure that your financial data remains protected from unauthorized access, theft, or loss. Quicken provides powerful tools to manage and track your finances, but your vigilance in securing your data is essential for maintaining privacy and preventing fraud. Make these practices part of your routine, and you can confidently manage your finances knowing your sensitive information is safe and secure.

Exploring the Quicken Mobile App

The Quicken Mobile App provides a convenient way to manage your finances on the go, offering users the flexibility to track, monitor, and control their financial life from anywhere. Whether you're at home, in the office, or out running errands, the mobile app brings the power of Quickens desktop features right to your fingertips. Here's an in-depth look at the features and functionality of the Quicken mobile app:

1. Overview of the Quicken Mobile App Interface

The Quicken mobile app offers an intuitive, user-friendly interface that simplifies financial management. With its clean layout, you can easily navigate between accounts, track transactions, and stay on top of your budget. The main dashboard gives you a snapshot of your finances, including account balances, recent transactions, and budget status, making it easy to stay on track without needing to access your desktop.

2. Tracking Accounts and Transactions

One of the core features of the Quicken mobile app is its ability to track your bank and credit card accounts in real-time.

- **Automatic Synchronization:** The app syncs with your financial institutions to automatically update account balances and recent transactions. This helps you monitor your cash flow and spot discrepancies quickly.

- **Manual Entries:** For accounts that aren't directly linked to the app, you can manually enter transactions, allowing you to track all of your financial activity.

- **Transaction Categories:** Each transaction can be assigned to categories like groceries, entertainment, or utilities, so you can keep a close eye on where your money is going.

3. Budgeting and Expense Tracking

The mobile app allows you to create and manage budgets wherever you are.

- **Set Budgets for Categories:** You can set spending limits for various categories and track your progress in real-time. The app helps you stay within your budget by alerting you when you approach or exceed your set limits.

- **Expense Overview:** The app offers a breakdown of your spending patterns, allowing you to see which areas of your life consume most of your income. This feature is ideal for adjusting your spending habits to meet your financial goals.

4. Bill Reminders and Payments

Keeping track of bills is essential to avoid late fees and missed payments.

- **Bill Reminders:** The Quicken mobile app lets you set up bill reminders to notify you when payments are due. This ensures you never miss a payment, helping you maintain a positive credit score.

- **Pay Bills Directly:** In some cases, you can use the app to pay bills directly through connected accounts. This feature makes paying bills a hassle-free process, allowing you to manage your finances from one place.

5. Investment Tracking

For users who track investments, the mobile app offers real-time access to portfolio performance.

- **View Investment Accounts:** You can view your investment balances and recent performance to ensure you're meeting your financial goals.

- **Track Stock Prices:** The app lets you monitor stock prices and other investments, providing insights into market changes and potential investment opportunities.

- **Investment Transactions:** Track your investment transactions and watch your portfolio grow (or shrink) over time, ensuring that you're on top of your investments wherever you go.

6. Cash Flow Insights and Financial Reports

The Quicken mobile app provides easy-to-read financial reports, making it simple to get an overview of your financial health.

- **Track Cash Flow:** The app tracks income and expenses, giving you insight into your monthly cash flow and allowing you to adjust your spending if needed.

- **Generate Reports:** You can generate detailed reports on your spending, income, and net worth, which helps you stay informed about your financial position and make data-driven decisions.

7. Data Synchronization Between Devices

The Quicken mobile app seamlessly syncs with the desktop version of Quicken, ensuring your data is consistent across all devices.

- **Sync Across Devices:** Whether you're using the desktop app at home or the mobile app on the go, all of your financial data is updated in real-time, giving you consistent, accurate information wherever you are.

- **Backup and Restore:** Your financial data is securely stored in the cloud, providing peace of mind that your information is backed up and easily recoverable.

8. Security Features

Given the sensitive nature of financial data, the Quicken mobile app takes security seriously.

- **Password Protection:** You can set up a password or use biometric authentication (fingerprint or facial recognition) to secure access to the app.

- **Encryption:** Quicken uses encryption to protect your financial information both while stored and during transmission, ensuring that your data is safe from unauthorized access.

9. Syncing with Multiple Financial Institutions

Quicken allows you to link accounts from multiple financial institutions, such as checking accounts, credit cards, loans, and investment accounts, for a complete overview of your finances.

- **Link All Accounts:** The mobile app gives you access to your bank accounts, credit card statements, loans, and investments, all in one place.

- **Track Multiple Institutions:** You can connect and track transactions from multiple banks or financial institutions, providing a comprehensive view of your financial life.

10. Alerts and Notifications

Staying informed about your financial activity is made easy with customizable alerts.

- **Custom Alerts:** You can set up alerts for transactions, bill payments, budget limits, or even low balances, ensuring that you stay up-to-date with everything related to your finances.

- **Notifications for Important Events:** The app can notify you when bills are due, account balances change, or budget limits are approaching, helping you avoid late fees or overspending.

The Quicken mobile app is an essential tool for managing your finances on the go. Its combination of tracking, budgeting, bill reminders, and investment monitoring features make it a valuable asset for anyone looking to stay in control of their financial situation. Whether you're at home, at work, or out and about, you can manage your finances anytime, anywhere. By integrating your financial accounts and data in one secure app, Quicken brings financial empowerment right to your fingertips.

CHAPTER 10

FINANCIAL HEALTH CHECK UP

A financial health check-up is just as important as any regular physical exam—it helps ensure that your finances are in good shape and on track to meet your long-term goals. Much like a medical check-up, it allows you to assess your current financial status, identify potential risks, and take proactive steps to address areas that need improvement. A comprehensive financial health check-up gives you an opportunity to evaluate key financial areas such as income, savings, debt, investments, and spending habits.

By regularly reviewing your financial health, you can spot any issues early, make informed decisions, and develop strategies to improve your financial well-being. Whether you are looking to save for a major life event, reduce debt, or invest for your future, a financial health check-up helps you stay in control and make adjustments to achieve your goals with confidence.

Evaluating Your Finances and Making Improvements

Evaluating your finances is the first step toward taking control of your financial future. It involves assessing where your money is coming from, where it's going, and how well you're managing it. This process provides a clear picture of your current financial situation, helping you identify strengths, weaknesses, and areas for improvement. Once you've taken stock of your financial health, the next step is to make informed improvements to set yourself up for greater financial success.

1. Review Your Income and Expenses

Start by thoroughly reviewing your sources of income and regular expenses.

- **Income Assessment:** Calculate your total monthly income, including salaries, business profits, dividends, or any other regular cash inflows. Ensure that your income is steady and sufficient to cover your expenses and savings goals.

- **Expense Tracking:** Take a look at your recurring expenses, such as bills, subscriptions, groceries, loans, and entertainment. Categorize your spending to see where the majority of your money goes. This will help you identify areas where you can cut back.

2. Analyze Debt and Loan Management

Debt can significantly impact your financial health, so it's important to understand where you stand.

- **Debt Assessment:** List all of your debts, including credit cards, loans, and mortgages, and calculate the total amount owed. Pay attention to interest rates and repayment terms. High-interest debts should be prioritized for repayment.

- **Loan Strategy:** Consider consolidating high-interest loans or refinancing options if applicable, to reduce your overall interest burden and free up funds for other financial priorities.

3. Establish and Track Your Savings Goals

Savings are the foundation of financial security and success.

- **Emergency Fund:** Ensure you have an emergency fund that covers at least 3–6 months' worth of living expenses. If you don't have one, start by building it up gradually.

- **Retirement and Other Goals:** Set specific savings goals for retirement, education, or major life events, such as buying a house or going on a vacation. Break down these goals into smaller, more manageable amounts, and track your progress regularly.

4. Assess Your Investments

Reviewing your investments is key to growing your wealth and achieving long-term financial goals.

- **Portfolio Performance:** Evaluate how your investments are performing. Are they aligned with your risk tolerance and time horizon? If not, consider rebalancing your portfolio by moving funds into higher-performing or lower-risk assets.

- **Diversification:** Make sure your investments are well-diversified across asset classes, such as stocks, bonds, real estate, and mutual funds, to minimize risk.

5. Evaluate Your Credit Health

Your credit score is a key component of your financial health, influencing your ability to secure loans, mortgages, or credit cards.

- **Review Credit Reports:** Obtain your credit report from all three major credit bureaus—Equifax, Experian, and TransUnion—and check for any inaccuracies or potential identity theft.

- **Improve Your Credit Score:** If your score is lower than you'd like, consider paying off outstanding debts, keeping your credit card balances low, and ensuring that payments are made on time to boost your score.

6. Budgeting and Spending Habits

Understanding your budgeting process and spending habits can make a significant difference in improving your finances.

- **Create a Realistic Budget:** Develop a budget that accurately reflects your income and essential expenses, while also allowing for savings. Use budgeting tools or apps like Quicken to track and stick to your budget.

- **Cutting Unnecessary Expenses:** Identify non-essential areas where you can reduce spending. Consider eliminating subscriptions or memberships you no longer use, cooking more at home instead of eating out, and shopping smarter to reduce costs.

7. Financial Planning and Setting Goals

Evaluate your long-term financial objectives to ensure they are realistic and achievable.

- **Set SMART Goals:** Specific, Measurable, Achievable, Relevant, and Time-bound (SMART) goals can provide clarity and direction. Whether it's buying a house, retiring early, or paying off debt, having clear, measurable goals makes it easier to stay focused.

- **Regularly Review Progress:** Regularly revisit your financial goals and assess your progress. Make adjustments as needed based on changes in your financial situation or priorities.

8. Seek Professional Advice if Needed

If you're feeling overwhelmed or unsure about how to improve your financial situation, consider seeking advice from a financial planner or advisor.

- **Professional Guidance:** Financial professionals can help you make well-informed decisions about investments, debt management, retirement planning, and tax strategies. They can also offer personalized recommendations to help you reach your goals.

9. Make Continuous Improvements

The key to long-term financial success is continuous improvement.

- **Stay Informed:** Regularly educate yourself about personal finance and money management. The more you know, the better equipped you are to make sound decisions.

- **Adjust as Needed:** Financial goals and circumstances can change over time. Revisit your financial plan periodically and adjust it to reflect changes in income, expenses, or life goals.

By evaluating your finances regularly and making targeted improvements, you can build a strong financial foundation that supports your long-term goals and security. The process of assessing your current situation and identifying areas of improvement may take time, but the rewards—greater financial stability, freedom, and peace of mind—are well worth the effort. With discipline, consistency, and a proactive approach, you can take charge of your financial future and make meaningful progress toward achieving your financial goals.

CHAPTER 11

PRO TIPS FOR POWER USERS

For those who have mastered the basics and are ready to take their financial management to the next level, it's time to dive into pro tips that can truly optimize your experience with Quicken. These advanced features are designed to help you streamline your finances, enhance your productivity, and unlock the full potential of the software. Whether you're managing complex investments, setting up automated workflows, or leveraging detailed reports for strategic planning, these pro tips will allow you to make smarter financial decisions and work more efficiently. In this section, we'll explore some of the most powerful, lesser-known tools and techniques that will elevate your Quicken skills and help you achieve financial mastery. With these tips, you can take complete control over your financial data and ensure that you're maximizing every feature Quicken has to offer. Let's get started!

Customizing Reports for In-Depth Analysis

One of the most powerful features of Quicken is its ability to generate detailed financial reports. However, the real magic lies in customizing these reports to suit your specific needs and gain deeper insights into your financial situation. Customizing reports allows you to break down data in a way that highlights key metrics, trends, and areas for improvement, giving you more control over your financial decisions.

1. Understanding the Types of Reports

Quicken offers several built-in report templates, each focused on different aspects of your finances. These include:

- **Income and Expense Reports:** These reports help you track how much money you're bringing in versus how much you're spending.

- **Investment Performance Reports:** A key tool for those actively managing their investments, these reports give insights into how your assets are performing.

- **Net Worth Reports:** These reports calculate your assets versus liabilities, giving you a snapshot of your overall financial health.

- **Tax Reports:** Quicken allows you to generate reports specifically designed for tax purposes, helping you track deductions, credits, and taxable income.

2. Customizing Report Filters

To make reports more relevant to your financial situation, you can apply various filters. Filters allow you to narrow down the data to specific categories, time frames, or financial goals. This helps in eliminating unnecessary information, so you can focus on what matters most. For example, you can:

- **Filter by Date Range:** Customize reports to show information for specific periods, such as monthly, quarterly, or yearly summaries.

- **Filter by Categories or Tags:** You can choose to include only certain categories (e.g., entertainment, groceries, or business expenses) or tags that you've assigned to transactions.

- **Exclude or Include Specific Accounts:** If you want to focus on specific accounts, like just your credit card or investment accounts, you can exclude other accounts for a more targeted analysis.

3. Modifying Report Layout and Format

Once you've applied the filters, you can further enhance your reports by adjusting the layout and format. Quicken allows you to modify reports to better suit your needs, making them easier to read and understand. Key options include:

- **Choosing Between Graphical and Tabular Views:** You can switch between graphical representations, like pie charts and bar graphs, or more detailed tables that show the raw data.

- **Adjusting Columns and Rows:** For reports that involve detailed transaction data, you can select which columns to display, such as transaction date, amount, account, or category.

- **Personalizing Titles and Labels:** Customize the titles and labels to better reflect the specific nature of your report. This helps when sharing reports with others or reviewing them months down the line.

4. Creating Custom Reports

If you need a report that doesn't fit into Quickens pre-built templates, you can create a custom report from scratch. Quickens customizable reporting feature allows you to select the exact data you need and present it in a way that suits your specific needs. Whether you're tracking business expenses, analyzing savings rates, or breaking down investment performance across different asset classes, custom reports give you the flexibility to focus on exactly what you want.

5. Saving and Exporting Customized Reports

Once you've customized a report to your satisfaction, Quicken allows you to save it for future use. This is especially helpful if you regularly need to generate the same type of report, such as monthly income and expenses, or quarterly investment summaries. You can also export these reports to other formats like PDF or Excel for further analysis or sharing.

6. Using Reports for Financial Analysis and Decision-Making

Customized reports are more than just a way to track finances—they are powerful tools for analysis and decision-making. By regularly reviewing your customized reports, you can:

- **Spot Spending Patterns:** Identify trends in your spending and areas where you might need to cut back.

- **Evaluate Investment Performance:** Track how your investments are performing over time and compare different asset classes or accounts.

- **Assess Savings Progress:** Measure how well you're adhering to your savings goals, whether that's for retirement, an emergency fund, or another financial milestone.

7. Automating Report Generation

For those who want even more efficiency, Quicken offers automation options for generating and sending reports. You can set up recurring reports that automatically generate on a set schedule—whether weekly, monthly, or quarterly. This feature saves you time and ensures that you're consistently reviewing your finances without needing to manually create reports each time.

By customizing your reports, you gain a deeper understanding of your financial landscape, allowing you to make data-driven decisions with confidence.

Whether you're trying to fine-tune your budget, track investment progress, or identify trends in your income and expenses, these tailored reports provide the clarity you need to achieve your financial goals. The ability to create, modify, and automate reports makes Quicken an essential tool for anyone serious about managing their finances effectively.

Automating Financial Tasks for Efficiency

In today's fast-paced world, time is a precious resource. Automating financial tasks is one of the most effective ways to save time, reduce manual effort, and stay on top of your financial obligations. With Quickens automation features, you can streamline many aspects of your financial management, from bill payments to tracking expenses and generating reports. By setting up automation, you can ensure that your finances are continuously managed without the need for constant oversight, allowing you to focus on other important areas of your life.

1. Setting Up Recurring Transactions

One of the most time-consuming tasks in personal finance is manually entering the same transactions each month. Whether it's paying rent, utilities, or subscriptions, Quicken allows you to set up recurring transactions for regular expenses and income. Once set up, these transactions will automatically populate in your account registers, eliminating the need to manually input them every time they occur. This ensures that all your monthly expenses and incomes are accounted for, without fail.

How to set up recurring transactions:

- Choose the transaction (e.g., rent, loan payments, subscription services) you want to automate.

- Set the frequency (monthly, weekly, yearly, etc.) and specify the start and end dates.

- Quicken will automatically add these transactions to your account registers, ensuring they are tracked and updated on time.

2. Automating Bill Payments

Managing bills is a crucial part of maintaining financial health, and missing a payment can often result in late fees or negative impacts on your credit score. Quicken integrates with various billers to set up automatic bill payments directly from your bank accounts. This ensures that your bills are paid on time, and you won't have to worry about forgetting due dates.

How to automate bill payments:

- Link your bank account to Quicken's bill-pay feature.

- Set up automatic payments for your regular bills (e.g., utilities, credit card bills, insurance premiums).

- Choose a payment schedule and ensure your funds are available to cover the payments when due.

3. Tracking and Categorizing Expenses Automatically

Manually tracking every expense can be overwhelming, especially if you have multiple accounts and spending categories. With Quicken, you can automate the categorization of your expenses by linking your bank and credit card accounts. Quicken automatically downloads and categorizes your transactions, so you don't have to manually enter or sort each expense.

How to automate expense tracking:

- Link your bank, credit card, and investment accounts to Quicken.

- Use the software's automatic categorization feature, which assigns each transaction to its appropriate category (e.g., groceries, dining, entertainment).

- If Quicken categorizes a transaction incorrectly, you can easily modify the category, and the software will remember this for future transactions.

4. Automatically Downloading and Importing Bank Transactions

Manually entering all your financial transactions is time-consuming and prone to error. Quicken automates the process of downloading and importing transactions from your bank and credit card accounts, saving you time and ensuring accuracy. These imported transactions are then categorized and added to your reports, helping you stay up-to-date on your financial situation.

How to automate transaction downloads:

- Link your accounts to Quicken using its secure connection to your bank or credit card provider.

- Set up automatic downloading for your transactions to ensure that Quicken regularly updates your financial data.

- Review the imported transactions and verify their accuracy, and Quicken will continue to download and categorize them automatically going forward.

5. Automating Investment Tracking

For those managing investment portfolios, Quicken can automatically track the performance of your investments, including stocks, bonds, and mutual funds. By linking your investment accounts to Quicken, you can monitor changes in market value, capital gains, and dividends without manually updating your investment performance.

How to automate investment tracking:

- Connect your investment accounts to Quicken.

- The software will automatically track the current value of your investments and provide regular updates on any changes.

- Use Quicken's performance reports to evaluate your portfolio's progress and adjust your strategy as needed.

6. Generating and Sending Financial Reports Automatically

Generating regular financial reports is essential for understanding your financial status and making informed decisions. With Quicken, you can automate the process of generating monthly, quarterly, or yearly reports. Once set up, Quicken will create these reports on schedule and can even email them to you or other stakeholders.

How to automate report generation:

- Set up a recurring schedule for your desired reports (e.g., monthly income and expenses, quarterly investment performance).

- Choose the report format (PDF, Excel, etc.) and select the recipients if you need to share it.

- Quicken will automatically generate and send the reports according to the schedule you've set.

7. Automating Financial Goals Tracking

Tracking progress towards your financial goals, such as saving for retirement or building an emergency fund, can be a daunting task without automation. Quicken allows you to set up specific financial goals and automatically track your progress towards them. The software can calculate how much you need to save, track contributions, and adjust for interest or investment growth.

How to automate goal tracking:

- Define your financial goals within Quicken (e.g., save $10,000 for an emergency fund).

- Set up automatic contributions from your linked accounts to fund these goals.

- Quicken will track your progress and update your goals based on the contributions and returns.

8. Utilizing Alerts and Reminders

Quicken also allows you to set up automatic alerts and reminders for important financial tasks. These notifications can remind you of upcoming bills, low account balances, or when a transaction is categorized incorrectly. Alerts help you stay on top of critical financial tasks without having to check your accounts constantly.

How to set up alerts:

- Customize alerts for bill payments, upcoming due dates, or important account balances.

- Choose the type of notification you prefer, whether it's via email, text, or pop-up reminders within the software.

- You'll receive timely notifications to ensure you never miss an important financial deadline.

By automating routine financial tasks, your free up time to focus on more strategic financial decisions, making your financial life more efficient and organized. With Quickens automation features, you can ensure your finances stay on track, reduce the risk of human error, and enjoy a more stress-free approach to money management. Whether it's tracking expenses, paying bills, or managing investments, automation simplifies the process and provides a clear overview of your financial health.

Syncing Devices and Cloud Integration

In today's digital age, managing your finances across multiple devices and platforms is essential for staying organized and efficient. Quickens cloud integration and syncing features allow you to access and manage your financial data seamlessly, whether you're at home, at work, or on the go. With the ability to sync your information between devices and store it in the cloud, you can ensure your financial data is always up-to-date and accessible, no matter where you are or what device you're using.

1. Syncing Quicken Across Devices

Quicken allows you to sync your financial data across multiple devices, including desktop computers, laptops, and mobile devices. By syncing your Quicken data, you ensure that your accounts, transactions, budgets, and reports are updated on every device you use. This gives you the flexibility to manage your finances from home, on the go, or from anywhere with an internet connection.

How to sync your devices:

- Log in to your Quicken account on your primary device (desktop or laptop).

- Enable cloud syncing in Quicken by signing into your Quicken account.

- Install the Quicken mobile app on your smartphone or tablet, and sign in using the same account.

- Your data will sync automatically, ensuring that your financial information is the same across all devices.

2. Cloud Integration for Data Backup and Security

One of the primary benefits of using cloud integration with Quicken is the secure backup of your financial data. By storing your information in the cloud, you protect it from potential data loss due to device failure or other unforeseen issues. Quickens cloud integration ensures that your financial data is always safe, securely backed up, and easy to restore when needed.

How to use cloud backup:

- When you enable cloud syncing, Quicken automatically backs up your data to the cloud.

- If you experience any issues with your device or need to transfer your data to a new device, you can easily restore it from the cloud.

- Quicken also encrypts your data during storage and transmission to ensure it is protected against unauthorized access.

3. Real-Time Updates and Collaboration

Cloud integration allows for real-time updates and collaboration between devices. If you make changes to your financial data on one device, the updates are instantly reflected on all other devices connected to your Quicken account. This is especially useful for households or small business owners who need to access the same financial information from multiple devices. With real-time syncing, everyone stays on the same page, and financial decisions can be made efficiently and accurately.

How real-time syncing works:

- Any updates made on one device (such as adding transactions, adjusting budgets, or generating reports) are instantly reflected across all connected devices.

- Quicken ensures data consistency by syncing changes in real-time, so you can always rely on accurate, up-to-date information.

4. Seamless Integration with Mobile App

Quickens mobile app is designed to complement the desktop and laptop versions of the software, offering users the flexibility to manage their finances on the go. The mobile app allows you to view your accounts, track expenses, categorize transactions, and even pay bills directly from your phone or tablet. With cloud syncing, all the changes you make on your mobile device are automatically reflected on your desktop version and vice versa.

How to use the Quicken mobile app:

- Download the Quicken mobile app from the App Store (for iOS) or Google Play Store (for Android).

- Sign in to the app with your Quicken account credentials to sync your financial data.

- Use the app to track your spending, view your account balances, and make quick updates while you're out and about.

5. Keeping Your Financial Data Accessible Anywhere

Cloud integration ensures that your financial data is always accessible, no matter where you are or which device you're using. Whether you're at home reviewing your budget or traveling and checking your bank balances, you can rely on Quickens cloud sync to provide real-time, up-to-date information at your fingertips.

How to access your data anywhere:

- Simply log in to your Quicken account from any device with an internet connection.

- Your financial data will be automatically available, including account balances, transactions, budgets, and reports.

- This eliminates the need for carrying around paper records or relying on a single device to access your information.

6. Keeping Data Safe with Encryption and Secure Login

Quickens cloud integration comes with advanced security features to protect your sensitive financial information. All data stored in the cloud is encrypted, ensuring that your personal and financial data remains private and secure. Additionally, Quicken uses secure login procedures, such as two-factor authentication, to further safeguard your account.

How to secure your Quicken account:

- Enable two-factor authentication for added security when logging into your Quicken account.

- Use strong, unique passwords to protect your account.

- Regularly review your account settings and security preferences to ensure that your data is well-protected.

7. Syncing With Financial Institutions

Quicken also allows you to sync your financial accounts (such as checking, savings, and credit cards) with over 14,000 financial institutions worldwide. This integration allows for automatic transaction downloads, so you don't have to manually enter every transaction. By syncing your accounts, you can track your spending, categorize transactions, and create accurate reports without needing to rely on paper records or manually importing data.

How to sync with financial institutions:

- Link your bank, credit card, and investment accounts to Quicken by entering your login credentials for each account.

- Quicken will automatically sync and download your transactions, providing a comprehensive view of your financial situation.

- You can also set up automatic categorization of transactions to streamline your financial tracking.

With Quickens syncing and cloud integration features, managing your finances across multiple devices becomes effortless. The real-time syncing ensures that your financial data is always current, and the cloud backup guarantees that your information is safe and secure. Whether you're accessing your data from your desktop, mobile app, or even a tablet, you can confidently manage your finances and stay in control, no matter where life takes you.

CONCLUSION

Congratulations on reaching the end of *How to Use Quicken*! You've taken a valuable step toward mastering your personal finances, simplifying budgeting, tracking investments, and optimizing your financial future. Managing money can sometimes feel overwhelming, but with the right tools and strategies, you now have the knowledge to take control with confidence.

This book was designed to guide you through every aspect of using Quicken efficiently—from setting up accounts to leveraging advanced features for investment tracking and tax planning. Whether you are a beginner or an experienced user, I hope you've found practical tips and insights that will make your financial management smoother and more effective.

I want to personally thank you for trusting this book as your guide. Your time and commitment to improving your financial habits are truly commendable. If this book has helped you in any way, I would greatly appreciate it if you could take a moment to leave an honest review. Your feedback not only helps others discover how beneficial *How to Use Quicken* can be, but it also allows me to continue creating valuable content to support you on your financial journey.

Your review can make a difference for someone looking to gain financial clarity and take control of their money. Please share your thoughts—it would mean the world to me and to those who are searching for the right guidance.

Thank you again for being part of this journey. I wish you success, financial stability, and peace of mind as you continue to make informed, confident financial decisions with Quicken.

Happy budgeting, smart investing, and all the best on your path to financial success!

Made in the USA
Columbia, SC
09 June 2025

59152474R00091